JAMES ✩ DEN

Shooting Star

JAMES ☆ DEAN

Shooting Star

BARNEY HOSKYNS

PICTURE EDITOR · DAVID LOEHR

CURATOR OF THE FAIRMOUNT JAMES DEAN MUSEUM

DOUBLEDAY

NEW YORK · LONDON · TORONTO · SYDNEY   AUCKLAND

Published by Doubleday, a division of
Bantam Doubleday Dell Publishing Group, Inc.
666 Fifth Avenue, New York, New York 10103

"Doubleday" and the portrayal of an anchor with
a dolphin are trademarks of Doubleday, a
division of Bantam Doubleday Dell Publishing
Group Inc.

Library of Congress cataloging-in-publication
data applied for

ISBN 0-385-41356-4

First published in Great Britain 1989
Bloomsbury Publishing Ltd.

All pictures supplied by David Loehr

Designed by Roy Williams and
Laurence Bradbury
Typeset by Bookworm Typesetting, Manchester
Printed by Butler & Tanner Ltd, Frome and London

CONTENTS

INTRODUCTION

'My life story seems so dull to me that I can't really tell it right without the Funeral March or 'Hearts And Flowers' providing a mournful background . . .'

Hasn't everything been said about James Dean? With Marilyn Monroe he is the premier prematurely-dead icon of the moving picture industry, the object, 34 years after his death, of a devotion bordering on the necrophiliac. Countless books, films, documentaries and special issues of magazines have been produced to explain why this legend endures and what exactly it is that he represents for a global popular culture. All of them tell roughly the same story of his brief, brilliant ascension and his sudden destruction, so why plod over the same trajectory?

Because I think none of these attempts has prodded sufficiently into what really makes this confused, narcissistic, violently ambitious, thoroughly inadequate boy so fascinating. Far more than being The First Teenager, as has so often been said, he is actually the first true pop star – the first performing artist to turn his life into an ongoing media pose. He lived life at one remove, the remove of a fame which couldn't have existed without celluloid and mass media. A sub-beatnik, would-be intellectual, pre-brat pack primadonna, he was the first truly 'pop' victim of the American Dream's star machine.

There was also something rivetingly touching about him, about his earnest re-invention and monomaniacal nurturing of himself as prototype pop original. He was King Baby in denim but he thirsted for something true and beautiful that only ever came in glimpses. As his Method-acting colleague Mildred

Dunnock put it, 'he was constantly at war with his own theatrical temperament, torn between the desire to be theatrical and the desire to be truthful.' Anyone who has ever wanted to *be anybody* in the post-Dean, post-Elvis pop universe must emphathize deeply with his quest. He was capable, too, of kindness and compassion, but these were always sabotaged by his egomaniac frustration and restlessness.

'Every day,' wrote Nick Ray, the equally restless (and ultimately equally mixed-up) director of Dean's most famous film *Rebel Without a Cause*, 'Jimmy threw himself hungrily upon the world like a starving animal that suddenly finds a scrap of food. The intensity of his desires and his fears could make the

search at times arrogant, egocentric; but behind it was such a desperate vulnerability that one was moved, even frightened.' 'He seemed to sense his own extra intuition and to see that it was of no use,' noted film critic David Thomson. 'His resignation and fatalism showed us the restricted personality of the world he inhabited.'

There is something a little mad, a little *possessed*, about James Dean. Each of his three major films conjures up a self-absorbed, hobgoblin kind of intensity. His is always a disturbing, albeit magnetic presence in the scene. Almost uniquely he can be viewed as something *apart* from the narrative flow, as if his Method-acting affectations create a space around

him that is separate and inviolable. (Dennis Hopper said that Dean's very shortsightedness meant that he was never really acting to other people, but always to himself.) In his 'private' life, too, he was always performing, carrying around a one-man show of attention-seeking antics and games that infuriated people more often than charmed them. He was the perpetual precocious adolescent trying to catch your eye while getting one over on you.

Dean has become more famous as an image, an *idea*, of nonconformist youth in the dead-dull Eisenhower 1950s than as a real actor. (Ironically, in *Rebel Without a Cause*, he ends up looking more integrated and sensible – less teen angst-ridden – than in either *East of Eden* or *Giant*.) How many 1980s teenagers have actually seen the three James Dean films? He may still make the pin-up-book shelves of the local newsagent (alongside Bros and Breathe and Brother Beyond), but is he perceived as much more than a beautiful icon, a mythical ghost whose image haunts jeans advertisements like a subtext? The very name 'James Dean' has become an artefact of cultural resonance in itself.

In one sense, because he lived his life with future biography perpetually in mind, Dean was an open book. Scarcely a day went by when he didn't contrive to have his picture taken in some new situation or activity. He wanted immortal love so badly that he turned himself inside out to beguile people; hence the apparently endless supply of anecdotes that survived him. Most important, he wanted to be famous for despising fame, for *not* playing the game like every other Broadway and Hollywood slave.

But if he was an open book for his biographers, was he not a mystery to himself? Was he not always chasing his own tail like a puppy? And so, one asks, in the true spirit of fan-dom, 'What was he *really* like?'

Let's try to imagine.

CHAPTER ONE

SMALL-TOWN BOY

'ATHLETICS IS THE HEARTBEAT OF EVERY AMERICAN BOY, BUT
I THINK MY LIFE WILL BE DEDICATED TO ART AND DRAMATICS.'

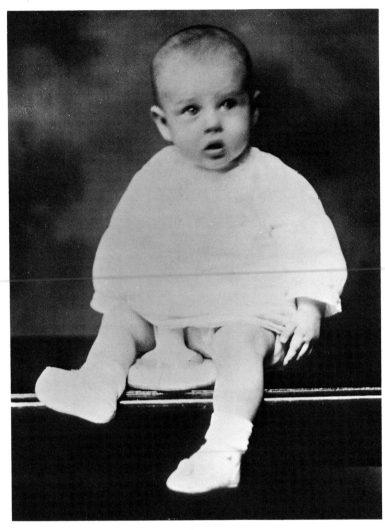

L ike so many American heroes, James Byron Dean came out of nowhere, otherwise known as the Midwest. Marlon Brando and Montgomery Clift, his principal prototypes, came from there; so, too, have Bob Dylan, Iggy Pop, Prince, Madonna.

He was born on 8 February 1931 in the Seven Gables apartment house, 320 East 4th Street, Marion, Indiana, 70 miles north of Indianapolis. His parents, Winton and Mildred, both of whom were natives of Indiana, called him James, after James Emmick – a colleague at the Veteran's Administration Hospital in Marion where Winton worked as a dental technician – and Byron, after Winton's friend Byron Feist – not, as has sometimes rather fancifully been supposed, after the English poet. Baby Jimmy weighed 8lb 10oz and the hospital bill for delivery was $15.

Winton Dean was a stolid Quaker whose Indiana ancestors could be traced all the way back to the *Mayflower*: 'emotionally remote' is an understatement and Jimmy never got properly close to him in 24 years. Mildred, on the other hand, was far from being a typical stolid Indiana Quaker's wife. If she hadn't quite heard of Lord Byron, she was clearly a very imaginative, probably very frustrated, woman determined on making her little prince somebody special.

James Dean was two years old when the family briefly left Marion and moved to rural Fairmount, about ten miles away. Winton's sister, Ortense, lived just outside the town with her former husband, Marcus Winslow, and they had a small cottage available for her brother. It was Jimmy's first stay in the town where he would grow up, if grow up he did, but it was not to be for long. Winton was not exactly attuned to rural life and soon took his wife and child back to Marion. In 1935, however, he was transferred to a VA hospital in Santa Monica, California, and the Deans migrated west.

The camera loves him: little Jimmy in 1931

Opposite: At three years old – not the prettiest little boy of all time

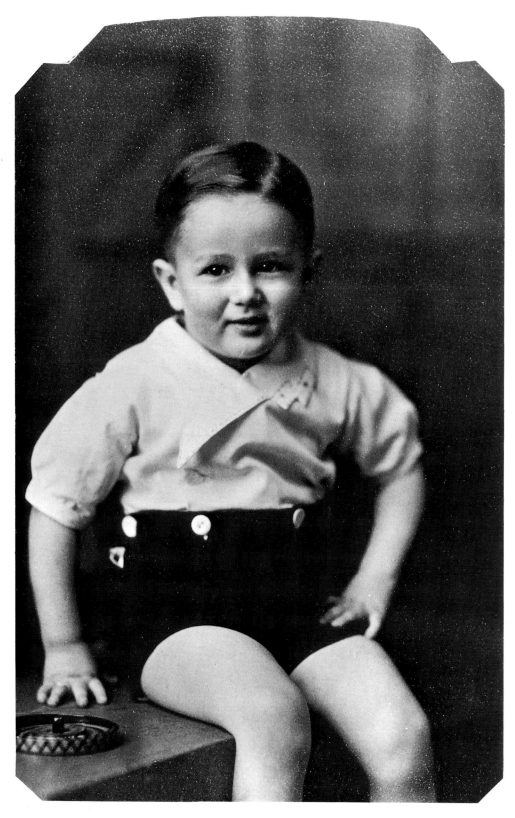

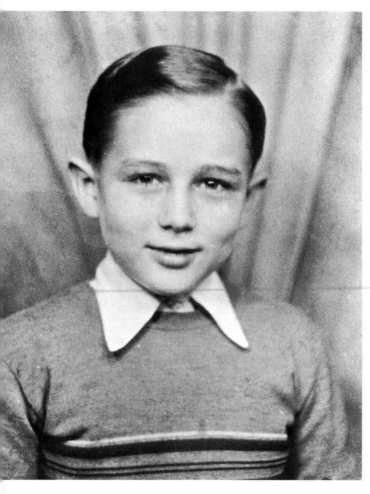

A better-looking twelve-year-old,
with elfin ears and outsize collar

Opposite: On the farm with his little
cousin Markie (Marcus Winslow Jr.) in
1947

Living in a cramped five-room bungalow at 814b 6th Street, Santa Monica, the uprooted Hoosiers slowly adjusted to the dream state of California. Despite her frustration with smalltown life in the Midwest, Mildred found Los Angeles artificial and missed her family and friends. Life became more and more centred on her sandy-haired, cherubic little son, whom she had playing the violin and tap-dancing by the age of five. Most significantly, she built the boy a little cardboard theatre and staged plays for his entertainment and education.

Like too many children with overzealous mothers, Jimmy was quickly teased when he entered the first grade at Brentwood Public School in September 1937. His Indiana accent and middle name were also predictable sources of mirth. Add to this a fairly delicate constitution – he suffered for some time from nosebleeds and internal bleeding – and the result was an acutely sensitive child in the making. Three years later, in April 1940, Mildred was dead from breast cancer, leaving the boy with a repressed sense of abandonment that underlined almost everything he was to do in life. Jimmy never fully recovered. Eight years later, as a high school senior back in Fairmount, he would write in a short self-portrait: 'I never knew the reason for Mom's death, in fact it still preys on my mind.'

Winton Dean, emotionally, and now financially, unable to look after Jimmy on his own, took his mother Emma's advice and, six days after his wife's death, sent the boy home to Indiana to live with Aunt Ortense and Uncle Marcus Winslow. Emma Dean had come out to California to be with her son and daughter-in-law in their agony and suffering. Now she was bringing the boy home, along with Mildred's body. At every stop on the train journey, Jimmy ran forward to the baggage car to check that the coffin was still there. It is almost unbearable to imagine. Indeed, there are scenes in *East of Eden* and *Rebel Without a Cause* – particularly the one in which Cal Trask is

Jimmy was a surprisingly good high-jumper and pole-vaulter. Here, at 14, he practises on the Winslow farm

dragged from his mother's office in *Eden* — where the viewer is virtually obliged to imagine the Oedipal intensity of his buried pain. Dean's famous outburst in a magazine interview years later — 'My mother died on me when I was nine years old ... what does she expect me to do? Do it all by myself?' — could almost be a line from that film.

'When Jimmy came back from California,' remembers Ortense Winslow — as good and golden-hearted a substitute mother as a boy could ever have hoped for — 'everyone bent over backwards for him. He ran all over the house checking that nothing had been changed. Someone brought over a little pony, and our daughter Joan let him ride her bicycle.' Jimmy spent the next nine years of his life in the Winslow farmhouse, built in 1904 on the rich black soil belt of Indiana's Till plain. If he was 'too pretty to be a boy', in Ortense's words, he grew up like a hundred thousand Midwestern country boys, helping out on the farm, fishing for carp and skating on the pond in winter, eventually learning to drive his uncle's tractor. When he'd got over, or sufficiently repressed, his grief for his mother, Ortense became 'Mom'. To all intents and purposes, too, Marcus became Pop — apart from occasional trips to California during school vacations, Jimmy scarcely saw his father in nine years.

Jimmy's relentlessness was apparent even at the age of ten. Always hurtling about on some new kick, he rarely stuck at anything long enough to develop it. 'He was never one to sit still,' remembered his cousin Joan. 'Always had to be the best at everything.' Schoolmate Helen Walters recalls him rigging up an 'elevator' from the top of the Winslow barn and almost breaking his back trying it out. On another occasion he lost his four front teeth after imitating a trapeze artist on a rope. (Pulling out his false teeth was to become a central item in his future repertoire of attention-seeking gimmicks.)

Two things, however, that he did persevere with down the

**Smalltown high-school photo in the
1946 Fairmount Yearbook (Jimmy in
centre)**

years were drums and motorbikes. Ortense, like her late sister-in-law Mildred, was always the first to encourage any of his emerging talents, and shortly after he entered the fourth grade at Fairmount Elementary in the fall she bought him a little drum. (She also arranged for him to have dancing lessons like Joan, and when he got straight As in his art class she sent him along to landscape painter Mary Carter: all of these things became important sideline outlets for Jimmy.) The introduction to motorbikes and a lifetime's obsession with speed and danger was initiated by Winton Dean's brother Charlie Nolan Dean, who often dropped by the farm and took Jimmy riding. For his eighteenth birthday, 'Mom' and Marcus bought him a small motorized bike called a 'Czech Whizzer'.

Jimmy later told the infamous Hollywood columnist Hedda Hopper – one of his great supporters – that he 'worked like crazy' on the farm, but only 'as long as someone was watching me'. 'The forty acres of oats were a huge stage and when the audience left I took a nap ...' (The memory recalls the scene in *East Of Eden* where he strives so anxiously to please his father in the lettuce fields.) Moreover, every situation was becoming a potential stage for the boy, and he frequently entertained the Winslows by mimicking relatives and friends. They also remember an extraordinary obstinacy, however. 'You'd try to order him to do or not do something,' remembered Marcus, 'and he'd just sit there with his little face all screwed up and closed ...'

Dean's theatrical bent was quickly spotted by Adeline Nall, who had started teaching drama at Fairmount High the same term Jimmy arrived at the elementary school. She remembers that he saw every play produced at Fairmount High from his fourth to his seventh grades, and that, encouraged by Aunt Ortense, he'd already given 'dramatic readings' for the local Women's Christian Temperance Union when, in seventh grade, he asked her to coach him through a melodramatic Victorian

Jimmy (wearing glasses) with track
team cronies, Fairmount, 1949

With bandaged finger (third from
right, front row) in Fairmount
Elementary school photo, 1940

On the edge of manhood, 1949, in the
senior class at Fairmount High

Left: The Fairmount High basketball
team in 1948, with Jimmy standing
second from left

piece called 'Bars'. The experience was an instructive one for Nall: the 18-year-old swore at her when 'Bars' failed to win him the WCTU's Pearl Medal.

During the war years, Jimmy Dean's life revolved mainly around 'one half mile of country road'. When not on the farm, he was to be found either at Marvin Carter's bike repair shop or at his pal Whitey Rust's house building go-carts. (Whitey would one day be a pallbearer at Jimmy's funeral.) Marvin Carter remembers Jimmy as a strange, intense boy who would come into his shop without saying anything. 'He'd just walk in and he might not even smile or say boo.' This was another habit that would continue late into his adult life.

Jimmy appears to have been neither introvert nor extrovert; he was too unpredictable to be pigeonholed in those categories. Nor did his thespian inclinations stop him partaking in such all-American activities as basketball and athletics. Although he was a mere 5 foot 8 inches tall and as blind as a bat, he proved to be a fine guard in basketball and – of all things – an outstanding pole-vaulter. 'Athletics,' he wrote cornily in his senior-year autobiographical essay, 'is the heart beat of every American boy' – even if, as he wrote elsewhere in the essay, 'I think my life will be dedicated to art and dramatics.' His basketball coach, Paul Weaver, recalls that 'Jimmy wasn't too coachable – I soon learned not to embarrass him in front of other boys.' Towards the end of his senior year, Jimmy notched up 40 points in three games.

If Fairmount was a more than fair approximation of the classic Midwest Anytown of Hollywood legend, the town boasted at least one genuine eccentric, if no certifiable rebels. James DeWeerd, the pastor of Fairmount's Wesleyan church, was as unlikely as his name, a former army chaplain from Cincinnati who had returned from the war a hero. Immensely knowledge-able and well-travelled, he knew about poetry, philosophy and

In the baseball team (second from right, back row), 1946

Left: Despite being comparatively short, Jimmy (pictured in 1948) was a dextrous basketball guard, and even scored 40 points in just three games during his senior game at Fairmount High

Below: At a football game in Fairmount, 1948

classical music, and cut a glamorous figure in the eyes of Fairmount High's more precocious pupils. He was, in fact, probably Jimmy's first intellectual hero, and introduced the boy to both bullfighting (showing him a film he'd shot in Mexico) and motor-racing. 'I taught Jimmy to believe in personal immortality,' DeWeerd later said. 'He had no fear of death because he believed, as I do, that death is merely control of mind over matter.' One can picture the adolescent Dean, sitting at DeWeerd's feet and soaking up his curious iconoclastic beliefs. The boy had probably never heard anyone, let alone a pastor, scorning Fairmount's smalltown ways.

By 1947, Jimmy was in his sophomore year at Fairmount High and on the Thespian Society's play-selection committee. In March he played John Mugford in *Mooncalf Mugford*, a 30-minute drama by Brainerd Duffield and Helen and Nolan Leary. Mugford is an old man who insists that the visions he sees by the sea are real. In the climactic scene of the play, he brings his wife down to the beach to show her. 'I can still remember Jimmy practically choking his wife into admitting she saw the visions,' laughs Adeline Nall. As with Jett Rink in *Giant*, the part called for Jimmy to play a man several times his age.

Several good roles came up for Jimmy over the next few terms. He appeared in W.W. Jacobs and Lewis N. Parker's 40-minute chiller *The Monkey's Paw*. In *Our Hearts Were Young and Gay*, he not only played the part of Otis Skinner, but also worked as assistant stage manager. In the fall of 1948, the first term of his senior year, he lost the lead role in Kaufman and Hart's *You Can't Take it With You* to Joe Eliot, playing Grandpa Vanderhof – the part made famous by Lionel Barrymore in Frank Capra's 1938 film – instead. He also featured in *Goon With the Wind*, a vaudeville-style Hallowe'en revue in which he played a rejected, vengeful villain in derby cape and moustache. Not content with this, he made the evening decisively his own

Portrait of an unlikely basketball
hero, 1949

when, at the end of the show, he careened into the auditorium made up as Frankenstein's monster. (For some years afterwards he talked of the power he felt as he stumbled around the audience terrifying everyone.)

In the spring of 1949, the term before he finally graduated, Jimmy made the front page of the *Fairmount News* when he came first in a 'dramatic speaking' contest in Peru, Indiana. His piece was the Madman's monologue from Dickens's *Pickwick Papers*, and the win qualified him to enter the National Forensic League's finals in Colorado at the end of April. Fairmount quickly rallied round to sponsor his trip, and on 27 April he set off for Longmont, 50 miles north of Denver, accompanied by Adeline Nall. Once there, Adeline urged him to cut the 12-minute 'Madman' piece on the grounds that its length would prejudice the judges against him. Jimmy, needless to say, wouldn't listen, but still shouted at her for not being more insistent when he was only placed sixth. (Some years later he was still sore enough about it to claim he had never bothered to go to the Colorado finals.)

A week later, on 7 May 1949, Jimmy went on a two-day senior class trip to Washington DC, and a week after that he graduated. He came twentieth out of 47 pupils in an exceptional year, won a prize as the outstanding art student, and took the medal for Best All-Round Athlete. A month later, Fairmount said goodbye to him with a touching farewell party, and on 15 June he boarded a bus for California. The smalltown years were over.

The Fairmount High Debating Society, 1949

CALIFORNIA DREAMING

'I'M NOT THE BOBBY-SOX TYPE AND I'M NOT A ROMANTIC
LEADING MAN . . .'

Jimmy was met at the bus station in downtown Los Angeles by his father, who was still working at the Sawtelle VA Hospital in Santa Monica. Winton Dean was doubtless as uneasy at the prospect of his son's moving in as Jimmy was. Four years earlier he had married a woman named Ethel Case, and son and stepmother had not exactly warmed to each other. Perhaps most important, Winton wanted Jimmy to go into law, imagining the boy would soon shake off his acting bug.

But Jimmy didn't shake off the 'bug'. Living with his father and stepmother on Saltair Avenue, near the hospital, he quickly sought out the local summer stock theatre company – the Miller Playhouse Theatre Guild – and registered for summer and fall sessions at UCLA, where he wanted to study drama. If the theatre company was (as he later described it) 'the most catty, criticizing, narcissistic bunch of people you ever saw, always at each other's throats', it provided him with a cheap education in stage management and gave him a walk-on part in a one-act play called *The Romance of Scarlet Gulch*. In the programme he was listed as Byron James, a name he considered using permanently.

Jimmy did, however, comply with Winton's wish that he study at Santa Monica City College rather than UCLA, and began his freshman year there as a physical education major in January 1950. (The college at the time shared grounds with Santa Monica High School, which, five years later would be used as the location for Dawson High in *Rebel Without a Cause*.) While he was there he was lucky to find in Jean Owen, chairwoman of the college's drama department, a teacher as sympathetic and alert to his talent as Adeline Nall had been at Fairmount High. Jean was the first of many mother figures to feature in Jimmy's life, and would often let him unburden himself of ideas and problems to her for hours on end.

Significantly, she also awakened his fascination with Hamlet, a role which – with its violent feelings of betrayal and abandonment towards his mother – must have held a special intensity for the young Dean. At the height of his fame he told Hedda Hopper that only a young man could play Hamlet; with older actors like Olivier, he said, 'you don't feel he is thinking, just declaiming'. Jean Owen recalls his interpretation of the role as being 'extraordinarily perceptive'.

Jimmy's social life during this period is not well documented, but apart from playing substitute guard on the college basketball team it is known that he often did announcements on the college FM radio station. With fellow student Larry Swindell, who says Jimmy 'fancied himself as a sort of Renaissance man', he would hang out at Ray Avery's Record Roundup on La Cienega Boulevard, listening to the latest jazz releases, and the pair of them would occasionally double-date in coffee houses like The Cave and The Point (on the ocean), cruising about in Larry's black Chevy coupé. It is possible that Diane Hixon, a willowy blonde, was Jimmy's first real girlfriend, but his friend and first biographer Bill Bast later wrote in *James Dean* (1956) that Diane quickly took fright at the responsibility of being a mother-substitute. He also joined another local theatre company, the Santa Monica Theatre Guild, and helped organize a May Day production of *She Was Only a Farmer's Daughter*.

At the end of his summer term Jimmy came home with As in gym and drama and Cs in pre-law. The grades said it all, and Winton gave way to his son's decision to enrol at UCLA as a theatre arts major that September. To help pay his tuition fees at the university Jimmy worked during the summer vacation as an athletic instructor at a boys' camp in Glendora, a suburb of Los Angeles just northeast of Hollywood.

With the move to UCLA came another move, perhaps equally important: Jimmy left his father's house and took a room at

As Malcolm in the 1951 UCLA production of *Macbeth*

Sigma Nu fraternity on Gayley Avenue. Although he wasn't the hearty fraternity type at all – 'he spent a great deal of time in individual endeavours rather than in cohesive activities', sniffed chapter president Manuel Gonzales, joining Sigma Nu was a necessary bid for independence, and Jimmy never again lived with family or relatives. One of his first friends at UCLA was Jim Bellah, son of novelist James Warner Bellah. 'Jimmy was the kind of guy who had to win,' remembers Jim, who for a few months became a fencing partner for Jimmy.

In October 'the biggest thrill of my life' occurred when Dean was cast as Malcolm in a big UCLA production of *Macbeth*, to be performed in the 1600-seat Royce Hall from 29 November through 2 December. Someone who remembers Jimmy's Malcolm to this day is Bill Bast, a man who over the remaining five years of Jimmy's life got as close to him as anyone did. Delivered in a pronounced Indiana twang, Jimmy's performance was, wrote Bast, 'like an agonizing dental extraction'. Bast instantly wrote him off as doomed to obscurity, little knowing that only a few days later he would be introduced to him by a love-smitten mutual friend called Jeanetta Lewis.

Bill was also from the Midwest, having transferred to UCLA from the University of Wisconsin, but felt very superior to the callow farmboy Jeanetta brought him to meet. 'He was very, very stupid for a boy his age,' Bill recalls, 'but there was also something quite strange about him.' For his part, Jimmy quickly recognized that he could learn from Bast and proposed, despite the lack of obvious rapport between them, that they room together. Things at Sigma Nu were coming to a head – Jimmy had started a fist fight with one of the house hearties – and excommunication seemed imminent. The two students roamed Santa Monica looking for an affordable place that wasn't too seedy. Both were desperately poor, though Jimmy supplemented his meagre funds by working as a projectionist in university classes. As they traipsed around, Bill began to see qualities in Jimmy that he himself sorely lacked – 'a strength, an assurance, a dedication, an independence'. 'The only greatness for a man,' Jimmy announced rather pompously the night they agreed to look for the apartment, 'is immortality.' Easy though it may have been to laugh at this earnest pretty-boy bumpkin, mugging up on culture and philosophy like Jett Rink improving himself on Little Reata, something in his tone suggested he was for real. 'It was astounding how fast he gathered information and education,' says Bill. 'It was as if he knew he didn't have much time to make up for the lack.'

Moving out of Sigma Nu – leaving an unpaid bill of $45 – Jimmy moved with Bill into a three-room Mexican-style penthouse apartment which they'd fallen in love with despite its comparatively high rent. 'I had the feeling the entire penthouse was suspended in air,' Bill wrote of the magical bachelor pad with its slanted ceiling and Aztec decorations. The first time Jimmy saw it he ran around like a little boy, touching and trying out everything he could see. This was *real* independence. Here the two thespians entertained, bringing girls home for candle-lit suppers and reading them passages from Henry Miller. Once, on a whim, they jumped into the '39 Chevy Winton had given Jimmy for his birthday and hurtled up to Santa Barbara for breakfast. But not every day was so high-spiritedly Bohemian. Bill Bast quickly realized that Jimmy was more than a little manic-depressive. When things weren't going well, he could retreat into a sullen silence lasting two or three days; then suddenly he'd be best friends again. It was a pattern of inconsistency and unpredictability that eventually wore Bill out.

Neither of them was exactly a conscientious student, except when it came to the theatre. In addition to majoring in theatre arts, Jimmy was ostensibly also studying geography, Latin American history, and general anthropology. But Joseph Birdsell, his anthropology professor, has no recollection of Jimmy attending a single class. It was clear to anyone who bothered to notice that he had made up his mind to act or do nothing. 'I don't even want to be the best,' he told Bill. 'I want to grow so tall that nobody can reach me. Not to prove anything, but just to go where you ought to go when you devote your whole life and all you are to one thing.' His first break finally came when his fencing pal Jim Bellah introduced him to Hollywood agent Isabel Draesmer, who promptly agreed to take him on, and his first job – two Pepsi commercials cast by New York ad man Ben Alcock –

His comical Indiana twang notwithstanding, being cast in *Macbeth* was the "biggest thrill" of Jimmy's life up to that point

**Outside the Santa Monica apartment
with Bill Bast's mother, 1950. She
came to stay and saved them from
starvation for another week**

came along in a matter of weeks, one requiring him to dance
round a jukebox with a group of teenagers. The other involved a
carousel and included Nick Adams (later one of Buzz's gang in
Rebel Without a Cause). For this piece of sustained Method-
acting genius he was paid $30.

Jimmy and Bill were invariably poor. Besides sitting around
the apartment scanning the *Daily Variety* and the *Hollywood
Reporter* for casting calls, the two of them would occasionally
work as ushers at the CBS Radio Workshop, a lowly occupation
but one which often led to useful contacts. Bill had got Jimmy in
at CBS, and Jimmy returned the favour by introducing his
room-mate to Isabel Draesmer. (Within a year, Bill had virtually
abandoned the idea of being an actor, settling instead on what
was to become a successful writing career.) Bill began to realize
that Jimmy was basically honest, despite an anxious desire to
impress that sometimes led to a certain flexibility with the truth.
Jimmy often bragged about his basketball skills and daredevil
motorbike antics; now success with women – more to do with
their falling at his feet than with any great powers of seduction
on his part – could be added to the list. 'These little pieces of ego
were never dropped with an arrogant attitude,' wrote Bill in
James Dean, 'but rather gently rolled over in his mind, as he
relived what had been to him remarkable and enjoyable
experiences.'

By January of 1951, Jimmy had more or less given up
attending classes at UCLA, justifying this with the grievance that
he had not been cast as the Witch Boy in a play by Howard
Richardson and William Berney called *Dark of the Moon*. 'I
couldn't take the tea-sipping, moss-walled academicians,' he
later told Hedda Hopper. But he *was* attending an informal
weekly acting class organized by the respected Broadway actor
James Whitmore. In fact, the class was Bill Bast's idea: knowing
of the legendary Actors' Studio founded in New York by Lee

Strasberg and Elia Kazan, he suggested to Whitmore that they attempt something similar in Hollywood. Whitmore agreed, on the condition that Bast round up eight or ten young actors for the classes. Jimmy was one of them, even though Bill had no grounds for supposing his friend would ever act any better than he had in *Macbeth*.

Whitmore was an avid exponent of the now somewhat notorious 'Method' school, based on the theories of the Russian Konstantin Stanislavsky. The Method required the actor to draw on personal emotional and psychological experiences in piecing a character together, and nothing could better have suited James Dean, who claimed that after meeting Whitmore he realized he *was* an actor – the question of deciding to *become* one was irrelevant. 'There's always someone in your life who opens up your eyes,' he said to Hedda Hopper. 'For me, that was Whitmore. He made me see myself. He opened me up, gave me the key.' When Jimmy came to Warner Brothers for *East of Eden* in 1954, Whitmore was on an adjacent set shooting Raoul Walsh's *Battle Cry*, and Jimmy made a point of going over to the set to thank him for his teaching.

Held in a meeting room above Brentwood County Mart, on 26th Street and San Vincente Boulevard, James Whitmore's classes were probably the closest thing Hollywood ever had to Lee Strasberg's teaching. In one class he had Jimmy and Bill enact a scene together, with Jimmy playing a thief trying to retrieve a stolen watch from Bill, who played a jeweller. Such was the intensity of Jimmy's Method-style involvement in the scene – his 'concentration', in Whitmore's terms – that the scene almost concluded in a fight. Whitmore had taught him that merely understanding the principles of acting was not enough.

In March, Isabel Draesmer sent Jimmy and Jim Bellah along to audition for a TV drama called *Hill Number One*, a rather laboured allegory for Easter which was being made by the Jerry Fairbanks Studio. In this teleplay, which was sponsored by Father Peyton's Family Theater, a group of soldiers in World War II suddenly metamorphose into Christ's disciples, debating, after their master's crucifixion, whether they should disband. Jimmy was cast as John the Apostle, the youngest disciple, along with Raymond Burr as Peter and Lief Erickson as Pontius Pilate. 'Was it for this we gave up our nets?' the youngster exclaims as they sit round a table. 'Just to go back to our boats again?' In a later scene in front of Christ's tomb, he shouts: 'He will bring us enlightenment! Come, we must spread these good tidings quickly!'

Bill Bast watched Jimmy's nervous tension build up before the shooting. Like most TV dramas of the 1950s, *Hill Number One* was going out live, and Jimmy was terrified. In the event, despite a heavy cold that made his voice sound unnaturally deep, he acquitted himself respectably, earning $150 and thereby just making his second rent payment. If the critics paid scant attention, such was not the case with a group of Los Angeles schoolgirls, whose prescient pubertal desires led to the formation of the Immaculate High James Dean Appreciation Society, the first of many fan clubs to come. Contacting Jimmy via Isabel Draesmer, the girls invited him to a party in his honour, to which – accompanied by Bill – he duly came. 'It was one of those embarrassing affairs where everyone just stands around a lot,' Bill later wrote. 'Jimmy got to play the star to the hilt and he loved it, and don't think he didn't take full advantage of the situation.' The Society later disbanded due to lack of funds, a predicament not unfamiliar to the object of their devotion.

There was a decided lull after *Hill Number One*, and Jimmy frequently sank into horrible depressions. In these states he would walk down to the Venice Amusement Pier at night, hanging out with assorted winos and weirdos until dawn. Bill soon learned that it was wiser to ignore him than to try and help.

In any case, when Jimmy finally came out of his depressions it was as though nothing had happened. An LA realtor who was an actor at the time remembers Dean on his nocturnal walkabouts: 'He was so beaten-down-looking, he looked like a teenage hobo. He used to stand around in Santa Monica with a hangdog look, or he'd be walking around eating a hot dog, just walking back and forth along the beach strip here.'

Someone usually came to the rescue when Jimmy and Bill were down to their last cents. Bill's mother came to stay for a week, filling up the larder and cooking for them every night. But Jimmy hated the feeling of obligation – as Bill says, 'he was always embarrassed when people did things for him'. Underlying all his depression was a determination to succeed without help, to prove to his dead mother that he could make it without her. One day, when Bill's mother was in the house, Jimmy worked obsessively on a mobile without saying a single word to her; by the end of the day she was a nervous wreck.

Jimmy was still stepping out with Jeanetta Lewis when Bill Bast introduced him to his own girlfriend Beverly Wills, an actress who played Fluffy Adams on a CBS radio show called *Junior Miss*. When the two couples first double-dated, Beverly thought Jimmy was 'pretty much of a creep' until he started talking about acting and Stanislavsky. By the summer she'd ditched Bill for him and was regularly filling him up with food at her mother's (comedienne Joan Davis) Bel Air mansion. Her eighteenth birthday party at the mansion – with guests like MGM starlet Debbie Reynolds, fresh from *Three Little Words* (1950) – was a major social event that year.

Bill Bast's heart was not exactly broken, but he was finding life with Jimmy increasingly difficult for other reasons. On a pedestrian level he was growing very tired of subsidizing him just because the boy was less keen on boring part-time jobs than Bill was. (Jimmy had been fired from the CBS ushering job which Bill

had secured for him.) More pertinently, Dean's violent mood-swings and all-encompassing self-preoccupation were becoming insufferable. When, in addition, Jeanetta Lewis discovered she was being two-timed by Jimmy, she and Bill decided to exit his life together. A nasty scene ensued when they arrived at the apartment to collect Bill's belongings, with Jimmy throwing a fit and hitting Jeanetta in the face. As they drove off they could see him standing in the street with tears in his eyes.

For a while, borrowing money from Beverly Wills and working as a parking lot attendant at CBS, Jimmy managed to maintain the penthouse apartment on his own. The parking lot job was not mere drudgery, as many a male starlet of the time could probably testify. The Hollywood film industry has always been rife with gay men, and CBS was no exception to that rule. Quite apart from being ambitious enough to exploit his physical beauty, he was narcissistically ambivalent enough to enjoy the sexual attentions of older men. When Rogers Brackett, 35-year-old director of the weekly radio show *Alias Jane Doe*, pulled into the parking lot one morning, the attraction was instant. Within weeks Jimmy had moved into Brackett's apartment on Sunset Plaza Drive, a steep road winding up into the Hollywood hills from the Sunset Strip.

Taking up with Brackett was a good excuse for breaking off with Beverly Wills, of whom Dean was rapidly tiring. One night at Paradise Cove, a trailer camp on the ocean near Malibu where Beverly's father escaped at weekends, he created a scene when he saw her dancing with one of the golden-haired, sun-kissed beach bums who made him feel so out of place there. Perhaps he was genuinely jealous; more likely he was looking for a convenient pretext for bailing out of the relationship.

Rogers Brackett got Jimmy work on *Alias Jane Doe* and *Stars Over Hollywood*, and this in turn led to bit parts in a few movies. Sam Fuller, who would go on to become one of the heroes of the

French *nouvelle vague* with films like *Underworld USA* (1961) and *Shock Corridor* (1963), was a friend of Brackett's and did him a favour by casting Jimmy as a GI in his Korean War picture *Fixed Bayonets*. As fate would have it, however, his one line in the film was later cut. In Paramount's *Sailor Beware*, an unfunny Dean Martin-Jerry Lewis vehicle, Jimmy played a second for Lewis's opponent in a boxing sequence, while another comedy, Douglas Sirk's *Has Anybody Seen My Gal?*, actually gave him some proper lines, albeit concerned only with ordering an elaborate ice cream sundae from Charles Coburn. The Sirk film starred Rock Hudson, whom Jimmy would come to despise so intensely during the making of *Giant*.

To his friends, Jimmy would laugh about his live-in relationship with Brackett, dismissing it as a meal ticket. 'It was a question,' in Isabel Draesmer's words, 'of marrying Joan Davis' daughter or going off to live with a studio director.' But he milked the situation for everything it was worth, and escorted Brackett to prestigious parties, private screenings, and expensive meals. Through a doctor friend of Brackett's, moreover, he managed to dodge the draft which had been looming over him ever since leaving Fairmount – by claiming he was homosexual. 'If it was a father-son relationship,' says Brackett of the affair, 'it was also incestuous.'

Brackett was an account supervisor at the advertising firm of Foote, Cone & Belding. One of his accounts sponsored *Alias Jane Doe*, and Brackett also directed that show: odd as it may sound, this was a common arrangement in 1950s Hollywood. With Jimmy, whom he wittily nicknamed Hamlet, he went several times to a gay club called simply The Club, just east of the Hollywood freeway on Hollywood Boulevard. He also re-introduced Jimmy to bullfighting – another sport which was to become an obsession – and took him to Mexico several times to see it. It was in Mexicali that they met director Budd Boetticher, who was making a movie called *The Bullfighter and the Lady*. Boetticher took to Dean and gave him a cape which had belonged to the legendary Brooklyn-born matador Sidney Franklin. It was something Jimmy would always treasure.

One time, back from one of these trips, Jimmy boasted to Bill Bast that he had fought a two-year-old bull; whether or not he believed him, Bill was amused to see that Jimmy hadn't shaken off his compulsive need to sound macho. Sitting in Barney's Beanery, a well-known hangout of industry hustlers and indigent actors, the drugstore matador settled his differences with Bill and brought him up to date on the James Dean story so far. Names were liberally dropped into the conversation, along with bitchy asides about the set Rogers Brackett moved in. In later meetings, the bitchiness had turned to outright resentment at the 'tap-dancing' he was expected to do – more than likely implying some demeaning favours. 'They think they're gods,' he told Bill, saying he was getting out of the Hollywood scene. 'At least I'll preserve some dignity.' In any case, he was getting hip to the fact that these favours weren't going to change the way he was perceived as an actor. 'I'm not the bobby-sox type and I'm not a romantic leading man,' he moaned. 'They'll never give me a real chance.' To create a new 'type' altogether he would have to go to New York.

James Whitmore had already advised a move to New York some months before, and now Jimmy was giving it serious thought. Coincidentally, Rogers Brackett was being transferred there by Foote, Cone & Belding anyway. And so it was that on 1 September 1951, James Dean kissed Hollywood goodbye and boarded a bus bound for New York, a city full of *serious* actors.

A wardrobe shot for Douglas Sirk's 1951 comedy *Has Anybody Seen My Gal?*, in which Jimmy's cameo role consisted of ordering an elaborate ice-cream sundae

CHAPTER THREE

BITING
THE APPLE

'HE WAS INSTINCTIVELY ABSOLUTELY RIGHT, BUT HE WAS ALSO
THE MOST EXASPERATING YOUNG ACTOR I EVER WORKED WITH
– SLOVENLY, LATE, UNSPEAKABLY DETESTABLE.' –
PRODUCER RUTH GOETZ

J immy made three stops on his journey East. The first was Chicago, where Rogers Brackett was working briefly. When Brackett realized Dean was serious about moving to New York, he called his composer friend Alec Wilder and asked him to book the boy a room at the Iroquois Hotel on West 44th Street. (Wilder, composer of Tin Pan Alley classics like 'While We're Young', lived next door in the rather grander Algonquin.) Jimmy's other stops were in Indianapolis, where he looked up his old mentor James DeWeerd, and Fairmount, where he stayed a few days with 'Mom', Marcus, and cousins Joan and Markie Jr, now six.

When Jimmy finally arrived in New York, carrying little more than $100 in his pocket, he was as overwhelmed and astonished by the city as any boy barely out of adolescence would be. So intimidated did he feel, indeed, that for several days he barely strayed outside his immediate neighbourhood, the theatre district, spending most of his time and money in movie houses. There, in the womblike darkness, he could forget how small and lonely and insignificant he was in the ultimate metropolis. Gradually, however, he overcame his awestruck fear of the giant buildings bearing down on him and began to explore the city, sometimes on his own, sometimes in the company of Harry Drake, the first of several photographers he befriended in his life. A restaurant called Hector's on Times Square, just around the corner, provided cheap food, and when the money ran out – it had come principally from DeWeerd and the Winslows – he moved to the YMCA on West 63rd Street and washed dishes in a bar on West 45th.

After a couple of weeks, Jimmy began making tentative rounds. Through advertising executive Jim Sheldon, a friend of Rogers Brackett, he got an appointment to see agent Jane Deacy at the Louis Schurr Agency. Deacy was no pushover but Jimmy instantly took full advantage of her maternal instincts, and by the next day he had an agent who was to represent him right up until his death. Adeline Nall, Jean Owen, and now Jane Deacy: three women of the theatre who all, in their different ways, mothered Jimmy.

In November, he got his first professional job in the city, testing stunts on an immensely popular TV game show called *Beat the Clock*. Hosted by Bud Collier, the show employed more than a few struggling young actors and actresses in its time, among them the great Warren Oates. Jimmy wouldn't rest until he had proved that the show's stunts – Collier's contestants were challenged to perform them before the clock ran out – were possible. If it wasn't exactly *Hamlet*, the work kept the wolf from his door. In the meantime he went up for as many open casting calls as he could; at the time there were as many as 30 live drama and comedy shows a week on TV, and all of them were produced in New York.

At one CBS audition at the Martin Beck Theatre, he met Martin Landau, an actor who was to become one of his firmest friends in the city. Together they would hang out at Cromwell's drugstore, an actors' coffee shop inside the Sixth Avenue entrance of the RCA building, or sit in Jimmy's YMCA room listening to Bach and Bartok. These were Bohemian days, and Struggling Young Actor was a 24-hour-a-day role.

Jimmy's first girlfriend in New York was a dancer called Elizabeth 'Dizzy' Sheridan. He met her one night while hanging around The Rehearsal Club, a rooming-house for young actresses and dancers, attracting her attention by reading out random sentences from a magazine in the club's lobby. It was a little-boy-looking-for-a-playmate seduction technique which was to become typical of Dean, and it worked. Dizzy remembers him as 'lovely' and 'intense' – 'he intensely spoke about intense things' – and their relationship was a very different affair from Dean's beach-movie summer idyll with 'fluffy' Beverly Wills. In

Dizzy he found someone who thought of herself as an artist and wanted to talk about books and ideas in West Side bars. It suited him perfectly in his attempt to become a hip beatnik intellectual. If he couldn't hit the road with Jack Kerouac, he could at least glory in the noble poverty of the suffering artist. As John Dos Passos put it in his poem 'The Death of James Dean',

> He developed a lingo
> out of tearoom talk about bebop
> and Bach
> and stale shards of Freud,
> existentialism
> and scraps out of translations of
> Jean Genet sold under the counter

Jimmy and Dizzy found a room together in the Hargrave Hotel, on West 72nd Street off Columbus Avenue. 'I washed his socks and underwear,' she says, 'and he introduced me to Shredded Wheat.' It was a close, ultimately suffocating relationship for Jimmy, but it lasted longer than most of his affairs were destined to. He would meet her after she'd finished a dance class or her part-time ushering shift in the Paris Theatre on West 58th Street, and they would adjourn to a coffee shop or, if they could afford it, to Jerry's, an Italian joint on West 54th where they felt at home. When Jimmy turned 21 in February 1952, Jerry's was where he gathered his new friends to celebrate. Among the people he was hanging around with were Alec Wilder, lyricist Bill Envig, actress Maggie McNamara, and Sir Winston Churchill's daughter Sarah, an early example of the hip English aristocrat in New York.

Rogers Brackett arrived in town just as Dean's financial state was once again nearing desperation. When Rogers found a studio on the top floor of a five-storey loft building on West 38th Street,

he invited Jimmy to move in, causing him guilt over Dizzy. She remembers him being terribly confused about his sexuality, and troubled over his relationship with Brackett – the two of them would often visit clubs on the West Village waterfront. Barry Strode, a production assistant on several New York TV shows at the time, says Jimmy 'courted around with a couple of TV directors, both gay, and lived with them a while', while another girlfriend, Barbara Glenn, got a letter bemoaning the fact that he was having to play 'street urchin' again. Significantly, Jimmy called sugardaddies like Rogers Brackett his 'mother hens'. When Bill Bast came to New York in the summer, he claims to have found Jimmy living 'under very unpleasant conditions' in the loft apartment. Jimmy used Bill's arrival as an excuse to leave, and the two of them hooked up with Dizzy Sheridan.

Twelve days after his twenty-first birthday, Jimmy finally got a bit-part in one of those TV dramas, playing a bellhop in a play called *The Web*. Even playing a bit-part he managed to antagonize producer Franklin Heller to the point where only the intervention of the director – significantly a woman, Lela Swift – saved him from being fired. Jimmy was already assuming the Brando-esque pose of the moody, perfectionist star, probably because he thought that was what the new, Angry Young Actor should do. The twin poles of his dramatic identity were Marlon Brando and Montgomery Clift – as he later shrewdly told Dennis Hopper, he had Brando in one hand saying 'Fuck you' and Clift in the other saying 'Please forgive me' – and it was common knowledge that he was obsessed by both of these beautiful, intense products of the Method school. (Both of them even claimed to have received bizarre phone calls from Dean during this period; obtaining their unlisted numbers would probably not have been difficult for an actor in New York.)

Not long after *The Web* went out live on 20 February, Jimmy *was* fired from another job, an episode of the private eye series

Martin Kane. No doubt his snobbish attitude towards television, common among 'serious' Method-style actors, didn't help. But Rogers Brackett came to his rescue once again, and in May he was seen in a *U.S. Steel Hour* teleplay called 'Prologue to Glory'. By the beginning of summer, Jimmy knew he could no longer put off what he'd really come to New York to do, which was to study at the Actors' Studio.

The prospect of auditioning terrified him. One afternoon he walked into Jane Deacy's office – by now he was calling her 'Mom' – and found an attractive blonde girl, Christine White, sitting at a typewriter. He soon coaxed out of her that she was writing a play. They got talking and went for a coffee at Walgreen's drugstore to discuss the idea of writing an original scene for an audition at the Actors' Studio. Christine wanted to study there too, but had intended to use a scene from Ibsen's *The Master Builder* to audition. Jimmy persuaded her to change her mind, and the pair of them set to work on a short script about two strangers on a beach.

For several weeks Jimmy and Christine rehearsed the piece almost every day, often performing it in bars and taxis or in Central Park for anyone who might care to listen. When on 12 November 1952 they finally took it along to the Actors' Studio on the 14th floor of 1697 Broadway – a stone's throw from where Dean had first touched down in the city – Jimmy was so nervous he almost bolted. Without his glasses he couldn't find centre stage and missed the spotlights completely. But the sketch, played in front of Lee Strasberg *and* Elia Kazan, was so mesmerizing that it ran way over time without anyone stopping them. And when they got the word from the Studio, they learned they were among only 12 successful candidates from the original 150 finalists.

Jimmy had attended only a few sessions with Strasberg before being heavily criticized for a scene he'd adapted from a novel by Barnaby Conrad called *Matador*. This was about an ageing matador preparing for a final, Hemingway-esque showdown, and Strasberg laid into him in front of an entire class. Jimmy stormed out, abandoning the house of Method just as he'd abandoned UCLA. 'If I let them dissect me like a rabbit in a clinical research laboratory,' he told Bill Bast, 'I might not be able to produce again.'

The event precipitated a long hot summer of depression and poverty, interspersed with moments of innocent happiness with Bill and Dizzy. After Jimmy left Brackett's loft, the three of them found a tiny apartment in an old brownstone on West 89th Street, the first of several places they shared that year. Clearly, Bill had put the past behind him – or else forgotten just how difficult Jimmy had been in Santa Monica. Life this time was equally tenuous – endless acting rounds (or 'cattle calls', as Martin Landau called them) and inedible meals concocted from the few remaining items in the larder – but time colours hardships with a nostalgic hue. In an apartment on the upper East Side, the trio didn't even have any bedding. One night Jimmy returned from Martin Landau's mother's house in Brooklyn bearing sheets and blankets. When he smugly prepared his bed, Dizzy and Bill tore it to pieces and all three collapsed in a heap of hysterical laughter.

One of Jimmy's favourite games was to play at bullfighting in Central Park – his experience playing the matador at the Actors' Studio hadn't cured his obsession. With Dizzy or Bill wearing a pair of horns he had acquired, he would stand poised with Sidney Franklin's bullfighting cape and challenge them to charge him. If he wasn't with them he would wander about the city soaking up what he called its 'violent fertility', studying the street life in all its teeming confusion and befriending eccentric characters like the blind classical musician Moondog, who walked the streets in full Viking regalia. This was all part of

Jimmy's cultivated identification with society's marginal people – the freaks, the deviants, and the dropouts. If he couldn't be a proper intellectual – and some time later he confessed to composer friend Leonard Rosenman that he actually had a problem with reading – at least he could be some kind of hipster existentialist, affecting solidarity with all species of noncomformist.

Bill Bast says Jimmy was always trying desperately to impress people, all because deep down he thought he wasn't interesting enough. Once he mugged up on two pages of Plato that Bill had referred him to, then later that evening launched into an exposition of Platonic Forms in the company of a film producer he wanted to impress. Almost the only book he ever quoted with any authority was Saint-Exupéry's *The Little Prince*, whose central message that 'what is essential is invisible to the eye ... one can see only with the heart' would one day be used on a memorial to mark the site of his death. However restless and self-preoccupied he may have been, Dean seems to have had a spiritual understanding of love as a force binding people together. But then aren't most fragmented, addictive people like Jimmy Dean often the ones with a real spiritual hunger for unity and wholeness? Should one laugh that Jimmy, of all people, would often warn Bill Bast to slow down because life was passing him by?

1952 was rolling by and nothing much was happening for Jimmy – with Paul Newman, among others, he had auditioned unsuccessfully for the role (eventually landed by Gordon MacRae) of Curly in Fred Zinnemann's film of the classic Broadway musical *Oklahoma!* He'd also studied a part in the TV series *Life With Father* for weeks, all to no avail. Then one afternoon, as a purely social introduction, Rogers Brackett took him to meet theatre producer Lemuel Ayers and his wife Shirley. Jimmy put on one of his best performances as a naïve but charming country boy, not even disclosing the fact that he was an actor, let alone a desperately ambitious one, and the Ayers liked him. In fact, they liked him so much that they asked him if he'd be interested in crewing as a cabin boy on their yacht one weekend. After winning them over to the main performance, convincing them that he could do this was the least of his problems.

Bill Bast noted that this new ability to ingratiate himself was a sign that Jimmy had matured slightly since his days in Santa Monica. It was only on a trip to Martha's Vineyard in September that Jimmy, who knew Ayers was casting a new Broadway play called *See the Jaguar* that fall, let the veteran producer know he was an actor. By then the friendship was so cemented that Ayers almost felt obliged to have him read for a part. The play, by N. Richard Nash, was described in its advance publicity as 'an allegorical Western without a horse', and centred around the character of Wally Wilkins, a teenage boy who has been locked up in an icehouse for most of his life. The part was tailor-made in heaven for James Byron Dean.

One night in October, while Jimmy was waiting to hear if he had got an audition for *See the Jaguar*, he and Dizzy woke Bill up and proposed they hitch-hike to Fairmount to spend Thanksgiving at the Winslow farm. Bill, who had a nine-to-five job at the time, said it was impossible, but Jimmy wouldn't take no for an answer and arranged for someone to let Bill's employers know that he was sick. By dawn they were at the New Jersey Turnpike with their thumbs in the air, and by the following night – thanks primarily to Clyde McCullough, a catcher for the Pittsburgh Pirates who was driving from his home town to Omaha, Nebraska, for a game – they were in Fairmount. 'It was extraordinary to see Jimmy in this home environment,' says Dizzy, who vividly recalls his tenderness around the animals on the farm. If 'Mom' and Marcus weren't too keen on them sharing a bedroom together, in all other ways their hospitality was overwhelming, and the three visitors took full advantage of the opportunity to fill up on Ortense's home cooking. A highlight of the stay was dropping in on Adeline Nall at Fairmount High and having her turn a theatre class over to the three of them.

The visit was cut short when Jane Deacy rang one morning from New York: Jimmy had been called for a proper audition and had to get back as quickly as possible. A week later he had the part in *See the Jaguar* and by 20 October he was rehearsing. The boy was going to be a Broadway star at the age of 21. For the next six weeks he drove Bill and Dizzy mad learning his lines in the apartment; worst of all, virtually tone-deaf as he was, he would lie awake at night trying to master a little folk song Alec Wilder had written for Wally Wilkins. Clearly the play was pretty terrible, as most of the reviews were quick to point out when it finally opened at the Cort Theatre on 3 December. An 'allegorical western' it might be, but its plot was so loaded down with portentous symbolic meaning that breathing any authentic life into it was almost impossible. Mildred Dunnock, a Method actress who had appeared with *Jaguar*'s star Arthur Kennedy in *Death of a Salesman*, remembers Jimmy grappling with lines 'so unbelievable they were funny'. 'This drove him up the wall,' she says, 'because he could smell falseness and artificiality.' Still, barefoot in overalls and wandering about the stage like a redneck *enfant sauvage*, Jimmy was sufficiently convincing to garner almost the only decent reviews the production received. There was enough of himself in the part, particularly in terms of his relationship with an over-protective mother, to work some pseudo-Method magic on it.

The fact that *See the Jaguar* closed after four nights didn't phase Jimmy in the least. He knew he was finally on course for the big time, and Dizzy could sense it too. 'He'd never doubted for an instant that he would make it,' she says, 'and now, while I

As the *enfant sauvage* Wally Wilkins in N. Richard Nash's *See the Jaguar*: on Broadway in December 1952, with Constance Ford and Arthur Kennedy

was still *schlepping* along, his mind was exploding with his future.' She knew their affair was on its last legs when Jimmy moved into the Royalton Hotel, directly opposite his old haunt the Iroquois. On the night of *Jaguar*'s opening performance, she watched him basking in his success at Sardi's, *the* theatre restaurant, and realized it was over. Not long afterwards, she left New York for a dancing job in Trinidad, and Jimmy began a series of brief and, for the most part meaningless, affairs that lasted until his death. If he was later deeply smitten by Pier Angeli, and if he was to battle passionately with Ursula Andress in the last months of his life, he never again 'settled down' with anyone.

The good reviews for *Jaguar* had made Jane Deacy's work in getting Jimmy parts a little easier, and the New Year brought a spate of roles in live teleplays. By this time Deacy had started her own agency and was looking to her golden boy to make it big. However, she knew better than to rush him, and even advised against his doing a screen test for MGM, whose New York office had expressed an interest in him. (She was still 'holding MGM off' in September, and Paul Newman eventually got the part in *The Silver Chalice* that they had wanted Jimmy for.) Nineteen fifty-three thus became Jimmy's apprenticeship year, a year spent in New York developing a relationship with the camera that would make him a movie natural and a year playing a series of edgy, unbalanced young men – all of whom almost certainly contributed to the making of Cal Trask (*East of Eden*), Jim Stark (*Rebel Without a Cause*), and Jett Rink (*Giant*). If fellow teleplay stalwart Kurt Kaszner was right in thinking that Jimmy 'felt so far above live television crap', the unfamiliar regular income wasn't exactly resented. (Jane Deacy was swift to suggest he entrust his money to her and live on an allowance.)

After two small roles in January (in 'The Hound of Heaven' on NBC's *Kate Smith Hour* and an episode of NBC's *Treasury*

Men in Action), Jimmy played Bob Ford in 'The Capture of Jesse James', one of a series called *You Are There!* Directed by Sidney Lumet, who went on to make *Serpico*, *Network*, and *The Verdict*, it gave Jimmy the perfect excuse to play with guns – which, as Lumet recalls, he loved. On 14 March he was seen in the CBS series *Danger*, in an episode entitled 'No Room' that starred Martin Kingsley and Irene Vernon. None of these episodes was preserved by NBC or CBS.

Having made some kind of name for himself in New York, Jimmy reverted to his old unpredictable habits. If he wasn't tearing around the city on a newly-acquired Indian 550 motorbike – often with some hapless girl clinging to his waist – he was busy indulging his ravenous appetite for physical and intellectual activity in a hundred restless ways, struggling to read books which would impress people, befriending all manner of freaks and oddball characters, and generally psyching people out with bizarre tests and mind-games. In actor Frank Corsaro he found another man whom he could drain for knowledge and enlightenment, and before long he was mugging up on Huxley, Kafka, and the impossibly difficult music of Arnold Schoenberg. Down in Greenwich Village he would hang out at the Minetta Tavern, the Louis Tavern and the San Remo, talking intensely with other actors and taking in the occasional European art movie. (He even took a small part in a downtown off-Broadway production of a play called *The Scarecrow*, featuring Eli Wallach and Patricia Neal.) When Bill Bast – called back to Hollywood to write for NBC – came to say goodbye, Jimmy gave him a copy of an *André Maurois Reader* inscribed with the words: 'While in the aura of metaphysical whoo-haaas, ebb away your displeasures on this. May flights of harpies escort your wingèd trip of vengeance.' The inscription was exactly the kind of clumsy sixth-form posturing in which he excelled.

Among the better TV parts that came up for Jimmy over the

following months were several that particularly suited him. In *Glory in the Flower*, a 30-minute play by Pulitzer winner William Inge, he was Bronco, a dope-smoking smalltown delinquent who anticipates both Cal Trask and Jim Stark; then a week later, in *Keep Our Honor Bright* (directed by George Roy Hill, of *The Sting* fame), he played Jim, a college student who in a subplot to the main story implicates other students in a cheating scandal as a way of deflecting attention from his own guilt. While both of these drew on his inherent instability, neither

Left & far left: In *Death Is My
Neighbour*, an episode of the CBS
series *Danger*. Co-star Betsy Palmer
was briefly a girlfriend of Jimmy's,
though she claimed he wasn't
interested in sex

of them used it to such pronounced effect as did Rod Serling in the Kraft TV Theatre play *A Long Time Till Dawn*, where Jimmy took a lead role as Joe Harris, a boy straight out of prison whose bitter conflict with his father only too obviously signals the film roles to come. 'There was an excitement and intensity about him that he transmitted viscerally to the TV audience,' said Serling of Jimmy, and in trying to make a comment about what he called 'the postwar mystification of the young, the gradual erosion of confidence in . . . a whole litany of moral codes', the writer found in the young actor a perfect embodiment of 'psyched-out' youth. Some years later he worked on a screenplay of *The Immortal*, from the 1958 novel by Walter Ross based on Jimmy's life.

On the set of 'Death is my Neighbour', an episode of *Danger*, in which he played a psychotic janitor and ended up being gunned down at a window, Jimmy met actress Betsy Palmer and began a short affair. She says he wasn't interested in sex, which squares with the impression Carroll Baker – later to work with him in *Giant* – had when she met him at the Actors' Studio: 'He was living with a girl (Dizzy?), but I always had the feeling that they didn't really do anything. As a matter of fact, my assumption about Jimmy was that he was almost asexual.' His longest relationship at this time was with a girl called Barbara Glenn, to whom he wrote several would-be intellectual letters, but by the end of 1953 he was squiring actress Arlene Sachs, who in contrast to Betsy Palmer seems to have enjoyed a pretty good sexual relationship with Jimmy.

By the end of the year, Jimmy had finally found an apartment for himself, a tiny fifth-floor walkup at 19 West 68th Street. A stone's throw from Central Park, it had – and still has – two porthole windows, making it feel more like a cabin than an apartment. It was the perfect Bohemian pad, a place where Jimmy always felt at home and where he entertained a diverse stream of actors, girlfriends, photographers, dancers and bongo

players. It wasn't enough for Jimmy to be an actor; he had to be all things to all his peers, and during this period he took on board as much as he could, learning photography from Roy Schatt, dancing from Katharine Dunham, and bongo-playing from black percussionist Cyril Jackson. (Dennis Stock's pictures of him in Jackson's bongo class in 1954 make him look like something out of a Roger Corman 'Beat' movie!)

Roy Schatt was one of several people who saw through Jimmy's desperate affectations. When Arlene Sachs brought him to Schatt's studio on East 33rd Street in January 1954, Schatt was not impressed. What he saw was a slouching, self-preoccupied, studiedly distant primadonna, and he'd already seen enough post-Brando 'existentialists' to last him a lifetime. Nor did his tolerance for Jimmy's behaviour improve with acquaintance. Nevertheless, as he admits himself, he became the first of many photographic Boswells to document the making of James Dean as we know him. One thing no James Dean lover could ever claim to be short of is pictures of him, and Schatt played more than his part in that. He also agreed to Jimmy's request that he teach him photography, helping him choose a secondhand Leica camera and showing him how to develop film. He soon realized how exasperating Jimmy's dilettante-ish attitude was going to be – the camera was just another toy, quickly tossed aside when the fun was over and the hard work of developing had to be done – but something about the boy compelled indulgence. One of his favourite pastimes was roaming the streets with Schatt and Marty Landau, shooting them from bizarre angles while Schatt reciprocated with shots of Jimmy.

In December, after a year of doing almost no theatre, Jimmy went up for a part in a Broadway adaptation of André Gide's *The Immoralist* and got it. Adapted by Augustus and Ruth Goetz, who'd been intrigued by the novel ever since Ruth had read it for

With Method actress Mildred Dunnock in *Padlocks*, another episode of *Danger*

its American publisher Alfred A. Knopf, its subject – hip on Broadway at the time – was homosexuality. A French archaeologist, played by Louis Jourdan, honeymoons in Morocco with his wife (Geraldine Page), only to find that their lewd, insinuating houseboy (Jimmy) can introduce him to the local gay scene. For Dean it was a role that called on all the sly charm and sexual ambivalence at his disposal, and he handled it brilliantly. Ruth Goetz remembers his audition in producer Billy Rose's office, on the top floor of the old Ziegfeld Theatre: 'He appeared in a ten-gallon hat and cowboy boots, bright green vest and jeans – he looked like a little Irishman. Then he began to read and he was instinctively absolutely right, charming but with a nasty, suggestive sexual undercurrent.'

He was also 'the most exasperating young actor I ever worked with,' as she quickly realized when rehearsals started on 18 December – 'slovenly, late, unspeakably detestable.' Billy Rose didn't care for him any more than Ruth did; Jimmy's relationship with him was like a rehearsal for his relationship with George Stevens on the set of *Giant*. On the train down to Philadelphia for a pre-Broadway three-week run, Rose told Ruth that if Jimmy didn't come through for them 'he walks'.

The last straw for Jimmy in the saga of *The Immoralist* was the replacing of director Herman Shumlin with Daniel Mann. Shumlin had been something of a father figure to him and had given him a lot of leeway and flexibility in interpreting the role of Bachir – one of the reasons, indeed, why Rose had fired him. With Shumlin gone, his only real ally on the set was yet another mother-figure, Geraldine Page. Furthermore, Shumlin's exit gave Rose the chance to cut many of Bachir's lines, with no word of protest from the new director, who in turn lost his temper so violently with Jimmy that he came very close to replacing him with understudy Bill Gunn. Only a run-of-play contract saved Jimmy from an ignominious exit. 'He had all these adolescent notions about being a man,' says Daniel Mann, 'carrying a knife, riding a motorcycle around … but it couldn't have nourished him very much or else he would have been much calmer and enjoyed it. I thought he was a very, very disturbed, very compulsive young man.'

When Jimmy hit the stage, all the aggro seemed to have been worth it. 'The first night in Philly we saw what we'd seen when he auditioned,' says Ruth. 'He was detestable backstage but completely pro onstage.' And it was the same when the production finally hit Broadway, at the Royale Theatre, on Jimmy's twenty-third birthday. Critics hailed what the *World Telegram* called his 'sleazy impertinence and immoral opportunism' and Broadway later gave him a Tony Award and the Daniel Blum Award for the Year's Best Newcomer. Only a few bitchy insiders carped that the role was too close to Jimmy's own personality to justify the term 'acting'.

On the night *The Immoralist* had opened in New York, Jimmy gave two weeks' notice that he was leaving the play. The Goetzs couldn't believe it – 'we ranted and raved and said it wasn't right and he didn't give a damn' – but Jimmy knew his time had finally come. Paul Osborn, who was writing a treatment of John Steinbeck's novel *East of Eden* for director Elia Kazan, had caught one of the play's Philadelphia previews and had called Kazan the next day to suggest he see Jimmy to size him up for the role of Cal Trask. This Kazan did the moment the company returned to New York for *The Immoralist*'s Broadway run, asking Dean to come and see him in Warner Brothers' New York offices. Remembering the temperamental boy he'd seen at the Actors' Studio, Kazan (or 'Gadge', as he was familiarly known in the business) wasn't wild about the idea – and was in any case thinking about using his original protégé Brando again – but he trusted Osborn's hunch. An hour after Jimmy ambled coolly into his office he knew he'd found his Cal.

Jimmy in *The Bells of Cockaigne,* a
1953 NBC teleplay in which he plays a
stevedore gambling his paycheck in a
desperate attempt to pay the
mounting bills from his child's illness

'When I walked in he was slouched at the end of a leather sofa in the waiting room,' Kazan wrote in his autobiography, *A Life*.

He was a heap of twisted legs and denim rags, looking resentful for no particular reason. I didn't like the expression on his face, so I kept him waiting. I also wanted to see how he'd react to that. It seemed that I'd outtoughed him, because when I called him in he'd dropped the belligerent pose. We tried to talk, but conversation was not his gift, so we sat looking at each other. He asked me if I wanted to ride on the back of his motorbike; I didn't enjoy the ride. He was showing off – a country boy not impressed with big-city traffic. When I got back to the office I called Paul and told him this kid actually *was* Cal Trask.

John Steinbeck used the very same words when Kazan sent Jimmy up to see him on East 72nd Street. As Gadge later told Hollywood columnist Joe Hyams, a friend of Jimmy's, 'he had a grudge against all fathers, he was vengeful, and he had a sense of aloneness and of being persecuted . . .' All of which made him an ideal candidate for the part – far more so than Brando or Montgomery Clift, who, ironically, also wanted it. In fact, as far as Jimmy was concerned, the whole thing must have seemed too perfect for words. Here was Elia Kazan, the godfather of Method and a film director who played the system by his own rules, proposing, at the very height of his own success, to take him to Hollywood and make him a star.

'People said Jimmy was like Brando,' says Kazan. 'He was nothing like Brando at all. He had very little pliability. He was just a very hurt person, and the main things girls felt, and boys felt, and faggots felt, was that they wanted to put their arms round him and protect him.' So convinced was Gadge that Jimmy was Cal, the terminally angst-ridden boy who despises his father even while crying out for his love, that he signed him up in New York before Jack Warner ever caught sight of him. And while Jane Deacy ironed out the details of the $18,000-contract, Jimmy had the time of his life flaunting the good news around town. Ortense and Marcus Winslow came to visit him and he played host of the big city, dragging them from one landmark to another. Doubtless he was a little too excited, however, because the week before leaving for Hollywood he took a bad 'spill' on his bike – not bad enough, unfortunately, to cure his macho fearlessness, but bad enough to write off the bike and kill his plan to ride rather than fly to the West Coast.

The hayseed Wunderkind's last thespian stand in New York before leaving was in an informal production of Sophocles' *Women of Trachis*, newly translated by Ezra Pound. Directed by Howard Sackler at the Cherry Lane Theatre, it co-starred Eli Wallach. Also due to work on *Eden* was the production's composer Leonard Rosenmann, one of the gang who ran around with Jimmy, Marty Landau, and Roy Schatt. Schatt came down to the theatre to take pictures.

On 8 March 1954, Elia Kazan pulled up outside 19 West 68th Street in a black limousine and picked up a dishevelled, bleary-eyed young hobo with a couple of brown paper bags for luggage. He took this creature to the airport and flew him to Hollywood, citadel of celluloid dreams. A year later James Dean was a major movie star.

EDEN

'UNLIKE MOST HOLLYWOOD GIRLS, SHE'S REAL AND GENUINE.'
SO SAID JAMES DEAN OF PIER ANGELI – BEFORE SHE BROKE HIS
HEART BY ANNOUNCING HER ENGAGEMENT TO SINGER
VIC DAMONE.

Jimmy's flight to Los Angeles – 'He kept looking down over the side of the fucking plane,' says Kazan – was his first time in the air, and as America unfolded beneath him, the director talked to him about Cal Trask, the delinquent farmboy in Steinbeck's quasi-Biblical story. Kazan and Paul Osborn had decided to use only the last sixth of the novel, concentrating on the relationship between Adam Trask and his two sons. Cal was Steinbeck's latterday Cain, bitterly competing with his brother Aron for his father's respect and love. If he doesn't quite kill Aron, as Cain slew Abel, he exacts revenge by taking his brother to see their 'lost' mother, who runs a whorehouse in Monterey.

Kazan told Jimmy he wanted him to put on weight and get a suntan: a boy working out of doors in Salinas, California, in 1917 would, he felt, look slightly healthier than this unshaven Bohemian from New York. Accordingly, he instructed Jimmy to spend a couple of weeks soaking up the rays in the California desert. When they arrived in Los Angeles at dawn on Thursday, 9 March, Jimmy went straight to Bill Bast's apartment and woke him up for breakfast – just as Bill had woken Jimmy in New York. Later that day they rented a Ford convertible and on the weekend drove out to Borrego Springs, 100 miles beyond Palm

Discussing his role in *East of Eden* with

Kazan

Springs. 'I couldn't recall ever seeing Jimmy in such serenely high spirits,' Bill noted later – despite Dean's affectation of indifference to his success. 'I just want to make this picture and get back to New York,' he muttered.

It was very important to Jimmy that Hollywood recognize how cool he was about his success. Partly to get his revenge for the way he'd been treated back in 1951, partly to fuel a sense of mystique about himself, he was determined on playing hard-to-get. Even with his West Coast agents, Famous Artists, he played things very offhandedly; fortunately, however, Jane Deacy had warned the company's Dick Clayton what to expect, and no one took too much offence. Warner Brothers had arranged for Jimmy to share a small $50-a-month apartment above a Burbank drugstore with Dick Davalos, who was playing Aron in the film. Davalos soon experienced his co-star's moodiness and unpredictability, and just as soon learned to ignore it in exactly the same way Bill Bast had. But the tousle-headed primadonna, the new Garbo-esque genius of Hollywood, wasn't satisfied until Gadge had personally taken him under his wing and installed him in a live-in dressing room on the Burbank lot. With Kazan living next door, one avuncular eye perpetually on his protégé, Jimmy felt as secure as anyone with a good manager does.

But he was lonely and sulked a good deal. Writing to Barbara Glenn in New York, he said he'd 'told the girls here to kiss my ass and what sterile, spineless, stupid prostitutes they are,' adding that 'I HAVEN'T BEEN TO BED WITH NO BODY, and won't until after the picture and I am home safe in NYC (snuggly little town that it is) . . .' The petulant, babyish tone speaks volumes, as does his first (wordless) encounter with the fearsome Hedda Hopper, one of Hollywood's two most powerful columnists. So intent was Jimmy on not playing the game that he was prepared to antagonize even this arch-dragoness of the gossip columns, slouching in his seat in the Burbank canteen without saying a

The 'new Garbo' in his live-in dressing room on Warner Brothers' Burbank lot

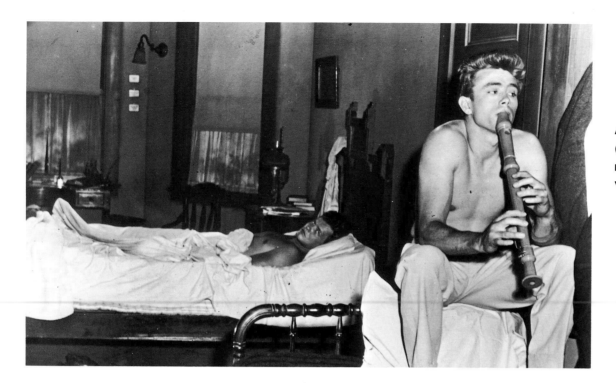

A faintly homoerotic shot of Jimmy (Cal) and Dick Davalos (Aron) preparing for a scene in *East of Eden* which was later cut

With *Eden* co-stars Julie Harris and Dick Davalos on location in northern California

word, then spitting at a publicity portrait of one of Warners' great stars which was hanging on the wall. Like Kazan's first encounter with him, it didn't leave her desperately impressed. 'To believe the press agents,' she wrote in her acid way, 'every dirty-shirttail boy in blue jeans who comes over the hill from Lee Strasberg's Actors' Studio is the biggest thing to hit the industry since Jack Barrymore played Don Juan' – but it piqued her

interest, and in due course, like one of Jimmy's many surrogate mothers, she became an avid Dean champion. On the next occasion that they met, Jimmy told her he'd wanted to see if anyone in Hollywood had the guts to write the truth.

Another woman with whom Jimmy had an interesting relationship was Julie Harris, the rather plain but marvellously gentle and understanding co-star who played Abra in *Eden*.

With Davalos and Harris on the *Eden* set at Burbank

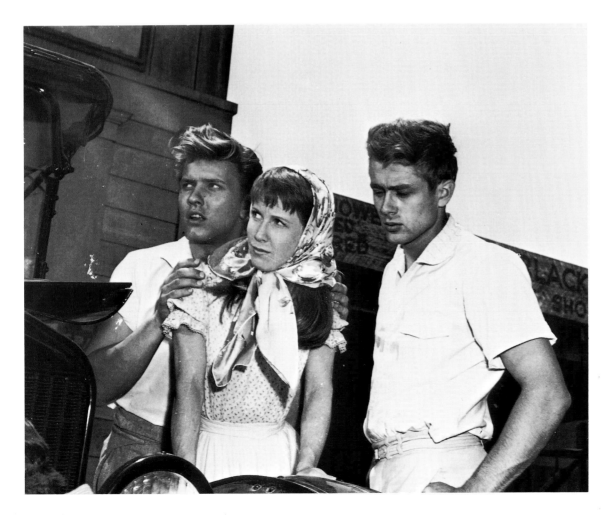

With the gentle and ever-patient Julie Harris on the set of *Eden*

Opposite: With Timothy Carey, who played the bouncer at Kate Trask's Monterey bordello in *Eden*

She'd made her name in *The Member of the Wedding* two years before, and immediately impressed Elia Kazan, who thought her face 'the most compassionate of any girl I've seen'. 'Jimmy was lucky to get Julie Harris,' says Kazan; 'he could have gotten a girl that just got angry at him and castrated him. He was easily castrated.' Gadge even claimed that Abra's gentleness was based on his own wife's love for him when he was, like Jimmy, an impossibly Angry Young Man.

On Julie's first night in Hollywood, Jimmy pulled up in the secondhand green MG TA he had just acquired and offered to take her on a drive into the Hollywood hills. Within minutes he'd hit 70 m.p.h. 'I knew enough not to say "Go slower",' she says, 'coz that would have been the red flag for him. You see, he was mercurial, unpredictable, always putting you on, which I didn't mind because he was very beguiling – there was something very sweet about him even though he was sort of a bad boy. He was like a Tom Sawyer to me ... he did manipulate people and he knew he was doing it.'

One of Jimmy's manipulations with Julie was to play mind-games on the set, asking her, for example, if she put her hands up to her face to make herself look younger. In his own way he was finding out how far he could go with her – a method of securing trust and forgiveness from women that he was to repeat with both Natalie Wood in *Rebel Without a Cause* and Elizabeth Taylor in *Giant*. Of the three of them, Julie was probably the most patient and supportive.

East of Eden finally started shooting on 27 May, beginning with exterior scenes – those set in Monterey – in Mendocino, on the northern California coast. By early June, location filming had shifted to the Salinas Valley south of San Francisco, where Steinbeck had actually set his novel; here Kazan shot the icehouse sequence and all the scenes set on the land around Adam Trask's farm.

A Brando-esque wardrobe pose for
East of Eden

Practising on the Salines fairground set built at Burbank

It was only a matter of days before Jimmy's need to psych himself up for scenes was severely irritating people. Most exasperated by his nerve-racking liberties and inconsistencies was Raymond Massey, whose personality was not so very far removed from that of the upright, stiffly honourable character he was playing. 'Simple technicalities such as moving on cue and finding his marks,' Massey wrote in his autobiography, *A Hundred Different Lives*, 'were beneath his consideration.' Kazan happily admits that he exploited this natural antagonism between 'father' and 'son' for all it was worth. Indeed, once they were back in Burbank and shooting on the Salinas set which had been built on the Warners lot, he actively encouraged Jimmy to put Massey's back up. To get Massey properly wound up in the famous Bible-reading scene, he told Jimmy to mutter obscenities instead of reciting the passages Adam had selected for Cal to read. 'You never know what he's going to do,' Massey would shout. 'Make him read the lines the way they're written!' When Jimmy threw his arms round Massey in the equally famous rejection scene, the older man was horrified.

More generally, Hollywood had never seen anything like

Playing director on the set of *Eden*

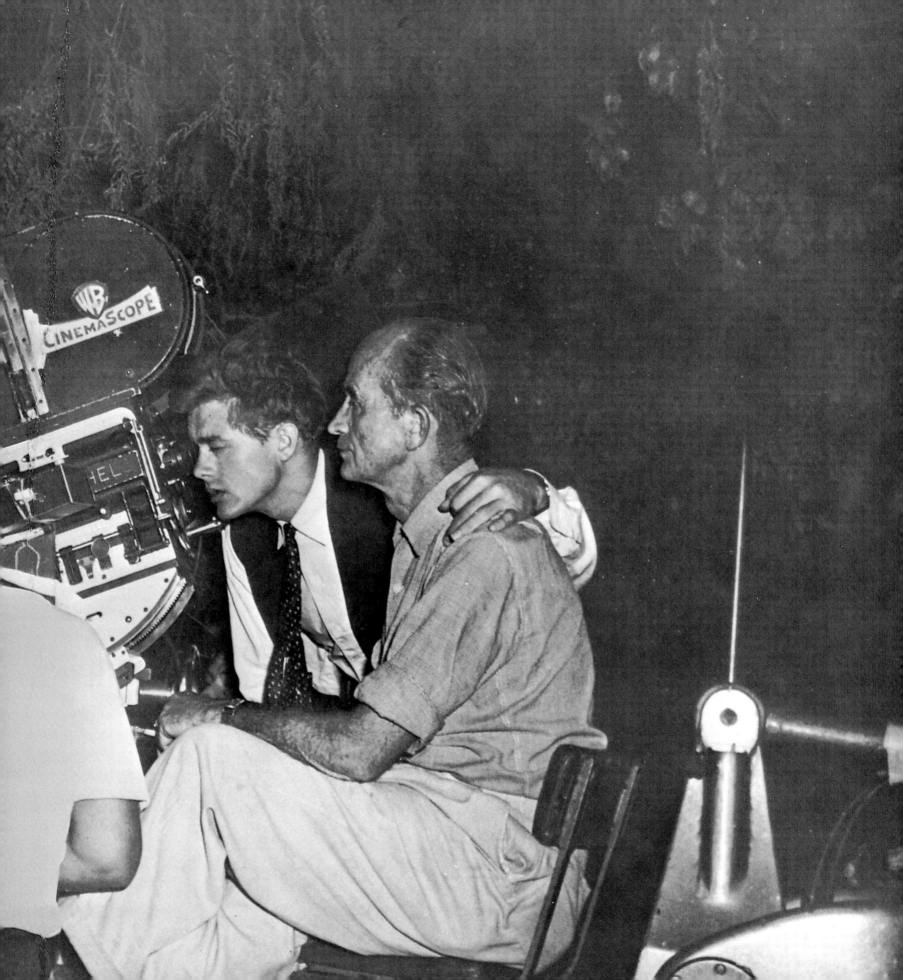

With Elia Kazan between takes.
Kazan was almost a surrogate father
to Jimmy, installing him in an
adjacent dressing room at Burbank
and keeping a protective eye on him
at all times

Opposite: A wardrobe shot on
location in the Salinas valley,
California

Jimmy. If Brando had been revolutionary in Kazan's earlier films *A Streetcar Named Desire* (1951), *Viva Zapata!* (1952, scripted by Steinbeck) and, above all, *On The Waterfront* (1954), Jimmy Dean was something else again. Even Kazan's crew thought the director was crazy when Jimmy screen-tested, and Jack Warner must have been flabbergasted. As Kazan says in *A Life*, 'Jack was used to Errol Flynn, Jimmy Cagney, and Gary Cooper. Now comes this twisted, fidgety kid from New York . . . ' But thanks to the Brando films, Kazan was flavour of the year at Warners and could do pretty much as he pleased. Warner let him get on with it. Even Kazan – after dubbing him with the nickname 'Creep' – drew the line at some of Jimmy's idiosyncrasies. Having been forbidden to ride a Triumph T-110 motorbike he'd acquired in case an accident jeopardized the production, Jimmy instead bought a beautiful Palomino horse called Cisco and arranged to have him kept on the lot. When for the umpteenth time he'd disappeared in the middle of shooting to feed the animal, Kazan banished it to a farm in the San Fernando Valley. With that gone, Jimmy proceeded to drive Gadge mad with his Leica camera – all the time, it must be said, worshipping Kazan as though he was the father he'd always wanted. Julie Harris remembers that Kazan gave Jimmy a jacket, and that Jimmy wore it night and day.

Elia Kazan had said that Dean *was* Cal Trask, and when the film finally came out the following year (1954), Jimmy's friends seemed to agree. 'There was so much of Jimmy in that film,' wrote Bill Bast, 'so much of the young man I had known for so long and had grown to love as a friend; so much of the lost, tormented, searching, gentle, enthusiastic little boy; so much of the bitter, self-abusive, testing, vengeful monster.' Back in Indiana, Adeline Nall recognized Jimmy's 'funny little laugh which ripples with the slightest provocation', the 'quick, jerky, springy walks and actions', the 'sudden change from frivolity to

COSTUME DEPT. PROD. 810
NAME JAMES DEAN
PART "CAL TRASK"
CHG.# 2   SC.51-66
EXT. RAILROAD YARDS

Wardrobe shot for the beanfield
scene, Salina valley

Wardrobe shot for a scene in the
bordello

Wardrobe shot for Monterey scenes,
Mendocino, California

Another wardrobe shot for the
beanfield scene

Between takes in Mendocino

gloom' – all of them 'just like he used to do'. Maybe he wasn't acting in any true sense of the word; perhaps the Method – the least methodical of all approaches to acting – had here reached its supreme embodiment.

From the opening sequence of *Eden* Jimmy is all petulant incoherence and fitful, jerking movement. His eyes are frightened slits in the glare of the sun. In his babyknit sweater and slacks he looks more like a little boy than any 23-year-old man

in cinematic history, and throughout the film he plays this little boy, appealing to the maternal instinct in all its female characters – even his 'fallen' mother. Where the men in the film in various ways dismiss him – Adam sighing 'I just don't understand that boy', brother Aron calling him a 'crazy guy' – the women are all disturbed and attracted by him. 'He scares me, he looks at you sort of like an animal,' says Abra (Julie Harris), who knows in her heart that 'bad boy' Cal is a more intriguing

Cal searches for his mother in Monterey. (Out-take)

specimen of boy-manhood than her lover Aron. Jimmy exploits his powers of seduction while all the time craving the love and approval of his father, the one person who is emotionally incapable of giving it to him.

Kazan's handling of the father-son relationship is uncharacteristically glib. To set us up for the rejection scene, when Adam declines the money Cal has made to offset his father's losses in a refrigeration scheme, he contrives a highly implausible change of heart on Cal's part – the result being a temporary period of love and trust between them which is all the more tenuous and precious because we sense it is about to be shattered. More authentic is Jimmy wailing '*Talk* to me', something he cries to both his father and his mother and a phrase which anticipates the Juvenile Hall scene with Jim Stark and his parents in *Rebel*. 'I gotta know who I am, I gotta know what I'm like,' he pleads to his father, and the words could have been Jimmy's own. Most real and most shocking of all is the almost primal scream he unleashes after his gift has been spurned.

Jimmy's presence in *East of Eden* accords exactly with reminiscences of his presence in the lives of friends and colleagues. He blows through the film like a small but highly charged storm, never still for a second. 'I realized there was great value in his body,' says Kazan. 'It was more expressive, in free movement, than Brando's. It had so much tension in it.' Like a hyperactive boy he is constantly in motion, swinging on a rope, dancing around his beanfield like a fertility sprite, climbing down from a ferris wheel and leaping into the fray like Peter Pan when a mob attacks the German shopkeeper Gus. In the jingoistic war parade through Salinas he tickles a girl, then pops a paper bag that makes a group of spectators jump. In conversation he is perpetually looking up, down, away, shifting from one foot to the other, while his voice drifts off on its own tune and tempo. In essence he is never really communicating

The father rejects his son: Jimmy's off-camera relationship with Raymond Massey (Adam Trask) was suitably uneasy

An artfully-staged Warners publicity
still

Cal struggles with Avra after
punching out his brother

Amateur stunts on the train to
Monterey

with the other characters; like a cross between an autistic child and one of the babyface psychotics he'd played in TV dramas, he is self-absorbed, self-contained, and self-imprisoned. When he asks his mother for the $5000 he needs to invest in order to make money for his father, he is so preoccupied with his own internal dramas that he fails even to perceive the irony of the situation. 'I don't have to explain anything to anybody!' he exclaims to Abra, and again the words could have been Jimmy's own.

By the middle of June, cast and crew had returned to Burbank for two further months of shooting. Here Kazan built a huge set modelled on the town of Salinas, complete with fairground and ferris wheel. (For the ferris wheel sequence with Jimmy and Julie, he borrowed a gigantic crane camera from the Disney studio and shot the whole scene with no fake backdrops.) Also shooting on the Warners lot at the time was *The Silver Chalice*, the film (about the Greek youth who made the silver chalice for the Last Supper) that MGM had wanted Jimmy to screen-test for in New York.

Starring in the film were Paul Newman – an arch-rival of Jimmy's in New York who had also screen-tested for *Eden* – and a beautiful young Italian actress called Pier Angeli (Anna Marie Pierangeli). Pier had been discovered at 16 by the director Vittorio de Sica and been brought to Hollywood to star in Fred Zinnemann's 1951 film *Teresa* (whose screenplay, incidentally, was by *Rebel* writer Stewart Stern). Meeting her one night with Newman and producer Joseph Wiseman, Jimmy was immediately entranced. Dressed like an Italian princess, with a face like a Madonna in a Florentine fresco, she was a vision of grace and aristocratic style completely out of his class. The only drawback was Signora Pierangeli, a mother as proprietorial and eagle-eyed as Brook Shields's. For this woman, and hence to a large degree for Pier herself, Jimmy was scruffy and non-Catholic and completely wrong for her precious, immaculate daughter. This

Avra with the more beguiling brother

Opposite: Cal and Avra on the ferris wheel in Salina

Between takes on the Monterey train

Cal with his mother (Jo Van Fleet) in Monterey

attitude, needless to say, made her the more gloriously alluring to Dean. 'Unlike most Hollywood girls,' he told a gossip writer, 'she's real and genuine.' Actually what he meant was that she wasn't another of the Tinseltown bimbettes with whom Famous Artists had set him up on spurious 'dates'. She was that narcissist's wet dream, the emotionally unavailable goddess.

Jimmy was as 'in love' with Pier Angeli as he ever was with a girl. For her he curbed his more reckless habits, opting instead for moonlit walks along California beaches. Raped by an American GI at the age of 15, Pier was not exactly relaxed in bed, but this probably suited Jimmy fine: he was more intrigued by girls who didn't want to jump into the sack with him. 'We were like kids together,' she said 14 years later, though whether either of these 'kids' was capable of loving the other is arguable. Elia Kazan wasn't overjoyed about the romance, since he feared it would cost him the miserable, narcissistic Cal he wanted for his movie. Often, too, he was kept awake at night by the sound of lovemaking or lovers' tiffs in the adjoining dressing-room.

With Pier Angeli, who shattered his
heart by doing the decent thing and
marrying Vic Damone

A picture that speaks volumes:
flanked by Elia Kazan and Julie
Harris, Jimmy's idol Marlon Brando
steals his thunder…

A testing moment came for Jimmy the day Marlon Brando, Kazan's first iconic hero, came on the set. Kazan recalls that Jimmy's voice would 'drop to a cathedral hush' when he talked about Brando, and that when the star of *On the Waterfront* was introduced to him he was 'so adoring he seemed shrunken and twisted in misery'. Jimmy may have sounded offhand about Brando on record – the picture of Gadge, Brando, Julie Harris, and Jimmy says it all, with Jimmy looking away, detached from the happy trio – but when it came down to it he worshipped the man as though he was an elder brother. When Jane Deacy suggested he distance himself from Brando's influence, Jimmy exploded, shouting 'Don't you think I'm aware of it?' Brando was his prototype, a devilishly sexy boy from the Midwest who rode motorbikes and played the bongoes – even if, as Kazan reiterates, they weren't alike. 'Brando had excellent technique, Dean none to speak of,' he says. 'In *East of Eden*, Jimmy would either get the scene right immediately, which was 95 per cent of the time, or not at all.' (When he didn't get it right at all, as in the scene on the slanting roof with Julie, Kazan would 'load him up with Chianti', a technique he often employed to bypass Stanislavsky.) Brando only made Jimmy the more abject by his patronizing attitude, advising him both to ease up on the daredevil motorbike-riding and to see a psychiatrist. (Jimmy was later cut to the quick when his idol told a reporter that the new kid in town had merely borrowed his old motorbike and bongoes.)

When Jimmy told Dennis Hopper that he had Marlon Brando in one hand saying 'Fuck you' and Montgomery Clift in the other saying 'Please forgive me', he came as close as anyone has to defining exactly what was new about James Dean. He was a synthesis of Brando's swaggering arrogance and Clift's troubled sensitivity, veering almost schizophrenically between the two. His friend Martin Landau says he was the first star really to

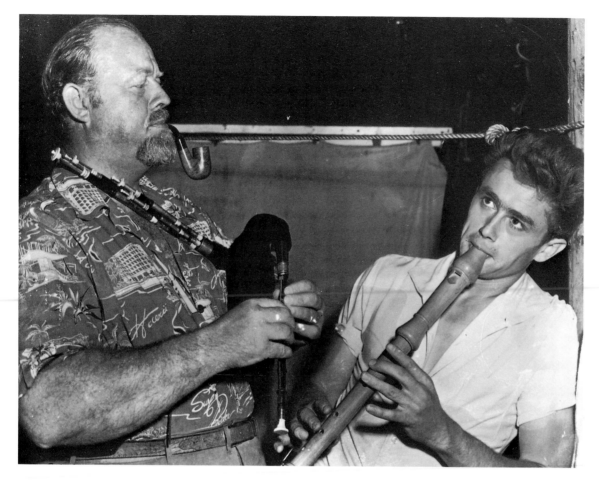

Left: Jamming with big daddy Burl Ives

Opposite: In the beanfield

overthrow the tough-guy gods of the cinema and define a new kind of masculinity – the first Hollywood actor to present a child's turbulent sensitivity in adult form. 'Before Jimmy,' he says, 'people only watched grownups in films.'

Finishing *East of Eden* was traumatic for Jimmy. Julie Harris remembers that on the last night of shooting in Burbank she went to say goodbye to him in his dressing-room. When she got to the door she heard what sounded like a little boy sobbing inside, and on entering found him with his head in his hands, tears streaming down his face. 'It's all over,' he spluttered. So thoroughly had he immersed himself in the film's world that the prospect of readjusting to reality was terrifying; so completely, too, had he turned cast and crew into a surrogate family that the idea of it breaking apart for ever was heartbreaking. Julie had

never seen a fellow actor so vulnerable. Who was the real Jimmy Dean – the boy who tore around the Hollywood hills in an MG, or this adject, inconsolable creature who wanted to be a celluloid Cal Trask for the rest of his life?

In August, with *Eden* behind him, Jimmy spent a fortnight in his beloved Manhattan, where Jane Deacy had got him a part on NBC's *Philco TV Playhouse*. The teleplay in question was another very routine melodrama called 'Run Like a Thief', but the chance to get back to New York was not to be missed. His New York cronies remember that he talked incessantly of Pier Angeli – or 'Miss Pizza', as he nicknamed her – and called her round the clock. Nevertheless, he listened to Jane Deacy's unsentimental warning that if he married Pier he would be known as Mr Pier Angeli, and that was not a wise career move.

Framing his green-eyed goddess:
Pier Angeli was emotional
unavailability personified

As much on his mind was the next major movie project marked out for him – a film ostensibly about 'juvenile delinquency' called *Rebel Without a Cause*. 'Whaddya got?' Marlon Brando had replied when asked in *The Wild One* what he was rebelling against, and here was a logical extension of that posture, with an irresistible title taken from a case history by Dr Robert M. Lindner. Ironically, the role of the book's disturbed teenage protagonist was originally intended for Brando himself, but the film never got made. When Nicholas Ray, a Hollywood 'rebel' himself, approached Warners executive Lew Wasserman with the idea for a movie about the growing restlessness of American youth, the book's title was resurrected. Production chief Steve Trilling asked Ray for a synopsis, based on interviews the director had conducted with judges and kids and social workers, and in September the film was given the go-ahead.

In October, while Warner Brothers were negotiating with Jane Deacy to extend Jimmy's contract to nine pictures in six years, Pier Angeli broke Jimmy's heart by announcing her engagement to a brutish Italian singer – and good Catholic boy – called Vic Damone. It was as impulsive and unwise as most showbiz engagements are, and within five years the subsequent marriage had ended in an acrimonious mess. In the late 1960s, not long before she overdosed and died of barbiturate poisoning in 1971, Pier was telling the *National Enquirer* that 'James Dean's Ghost Wrecked My Two Marriages', claiming that he was the only man she had ever 'loved deeply as a woman should love a man'. Of course, the chances are that a marriage to Jimmy would have ended up the same way. Lenny Rosenman, the New York composer friend whom Jimmy had persuaded Elia Kazan to use on *East of Eden*, remembers Jimmy being drunkenly violent with girlfriends, and says Jimmy confessed to him that he beat up Pier a few nights before her marriage on 24 November. Perhaps this was the incident referred to by *Herald Tribune* Hollywood columnist Joe Hyams, who had befriended Jimmy at the inception of the romance. Turning up outside a little apartment Jimmy was renting on Sunset Plaza Drive – 'a wastebasket with walls', Jimmy called it – he saw a tear-stained Pier driving away and found the actor distraught inside. Pier had told him she was pregnant. Some days after the marriage – in the very church where Jimmy and Pier had themselves planned to marry – Hyams found Jimmy huddled in a dark corner of the apartment, cradling a picture of Pier in his hands. The weeping boy couldn't even acknowledge Hyams's presence.

With his dream of ideal love shattered, Jimmy no longer had any reason to behave himself, and began living the Hollywood nightlife along the Sunset Strip, meeting every midnight at Googie's coffee bar with a group of cronies who became known as 'The Night Watch'. At the centre of this 'crew of creeps', as one gossip writer described them, was an eccentric creature called Vampira, who introduced horror movies on TV and studied the occult. Born Maila Nurmi in Finland, she was nearly ten years older than Jimmy and the other actors who hung around her. 'I had studied *The Golden Bough* and de Sade,' Jimmy rather pompously informed Hedda Hopper some time later, 'and I was interested in finding out if this girl was obsessed by a satanic force. She knew absolutely nothing. I found her void of any interest except her Vampira makeup.' At the time, however, she was an engaging fruitfly who led the crew on a merry crawl of 'coffee-*klatsch*ing' from Googie's to Schwab's and on to Barney's Beanery. In actor Jack Simmons's Cadillac hearse, they would ride around Hollywood talking about death. Bill Bast sometimes came across the 'Watch' at play, indulging in the sort of 'weird mood games' to which Jimmy had resorted ever since Bill had known him. As he watched them slouched around a table in Googie's, trying to out-psych everyone around them, he quickly tired of their Sunset-Strip existentialism.

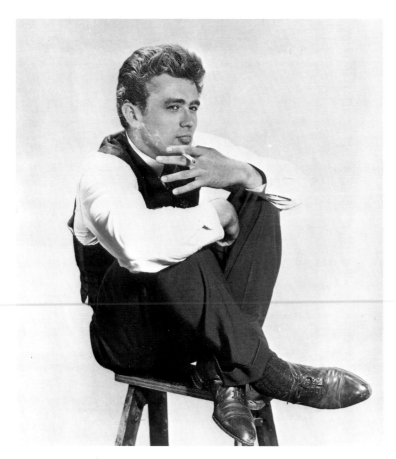

**A publicity shot for the movie
magazines**

In December, before heading east once more for Christmas, Jimmy appeared in 'The Dark, Dark Hours' and 'I Am a Fool', both *General Electric Theatre* teleplays. In the first he was yet another hipster psychopath, breaking into doctor Ronald Reagan's house and demanding medical attention for his wounded buddy. Many today would doubtless derive enormous pleasure from watching Jimmy point a gun at Reagan, who said he was 'struck by how very much James Dean off-camera resembled James Dean on-camera'. 'He worked very hard at his craft,' added Reagan, 'rehearsing with the same intensity as on camera and going almost all out any time he read his lines.' In 'I

Am a Fool', meanwhile, he worked for the first time with Natalie Wood, not yet certain for the part of Judy in *Rebel Without a Cause*. Only 16 but already a veteran child star, she'd been forewarned of his eccentricities and immediately endeared herself to him by saying that being a child star was better than acting like a baby. Adapted from a Sherwood Anderson short story, the play was about an old man (Eddie Albert) remembering how he lost the love of his life through his pathological lies. Jimmy played the Albert character as a young man in flashback and Natalie the girl he loses through pretending to be someone he isn't.

When Warner Brothers announced on 4 January 1955 that he was to play Jim Stark in *Rebel Without a Cause*, Jimmy was once again back in New York, having spent a white Christmas with the Winslows. Apart from running around town with his usual crowd – Marty Landau, Bob Heller, Barbara Glenn, Billy Gunn, and Roy Schatt – he appeared with Mary Astor in a *U.S. Steel Hour* teleplay called 'The Thief', playing the younger son of a rich family who is suspected of stealing. Astor liked him, but both she and Paul Lukas found it impossible to hear what he was saying, a common complaint from seasoned actors unaccustomed to the mumbling delivery of young Methodites. Roy Schatt came on the set and shot pictures of Jimmy clowning in rehearsal – in one of them, Jimmy pushed his glasses to the right of his face and shouted 'Hey Roy! I'm a Picasso!' (The remark referred back to a day when Jimmy had asked Schatt to explain Picasso's simultaneous perspective to him.) It was at this time, too, that Schatt took the famous portraits of Jimmy which became known as the 'Torn Sweater' series – 16 pictures of our hero in his best unshaven Michelangelo's-David-on-the-Left-Bank guise.

Desperate to get his face into the pages of the esteemed magazine *Life*, Jimmy hoped these shots would do the trick. In the event, he had to wait another month before *Life* was

With Dennis Stock at the Fairmount High Valentine Dance, 1955. More than any other photographer, Stock enabled Jimmy to mythologize himself as an enigmatic beatnik genius

A local hero signs autographs at the Valentine Dance

sufficiently interested in him to consider devoting a whole photo-essay to the 'Moody New Star'. The photographer in question was Dennis Stock, whom he met at one of Nick Ray's informal Sunday parties in his Chateau Marmont bungalow and who, together with Bill Bast and a new Hollywood soulmate called Lew Bracker, was one of the privileged few Jimmy invited to see the first preview of *East of Eden*.

For Stock — as inevitably it was for Bill — Jimmy's performance in the film was an extraordinary revelation. 'There was no question that a star was born with the first public screening of *East of Eden*,' he later wrote, 'for the entire audience applauded loudly as the house lights signalled the end. It took a few moments for me to reconcile the image of Cal with that of the unimposing, reserved young man I had met the previous Sunday. What I knew was that I had to do a story on James Dean.' The

two met for breakfast at Googie's the next morning and discussed ideas for the story, which was to 'reveal the environments that affected and shaped the unique character of James Byron Dean'. The 'story', which eventually ran in *Life* on 7 March, was a crowning moment in Jimmy's myth-making self-promotion. For two weeks, as the pair stayed in Fairmount, travelled on to New York, and finally returned to Hollywood, Stock was as faithful a Boswell as Jimmy Dean ever had. 'By now,' Stock noted, 'there was ever-increasing interest in the new star as the press became more and more aware of *East of Eden*. The upshot of Jimmy's increasing popularity was reflected in the new stipulations he tried to enforce on the *Life* coverage. At one point he insisted on a cover guarantee and the hiring of a friend of his to write the text. It was an unusual and highly egocentric gesture.' Stock never actually passed on these stipulations,

On the *Eden* set at Burbank

On the Warners backlot, Burbank

A tormented test shot from
East Of Eden

knowing that if they were enforced the magazine's editors might well drop the piece altogether.

Though the photographs are brilliant, they fail to conceal the artful contrivance of their context. Many of them – Jimmy playing his bongoes in a field of pigs and cows, Jimmy reading the old Indiana poet James Whitcomb Riley at the breakfast table, Jimmy pacing in the rain through Times Square, Jimmy in the Actors' Studio – have become part-and-parcel of his iconography, which is precisely the intention behind them. As a collection they could be entitled 'The Many Sides and Manifold Uncategorizability of James Byron Dean'. Here he is, a modern Renaissance punk getting his Warholian 15-minutes' worth, the crucial point being that he is *not just another actor*. From a Fairmount farmhouse to a Manhattan dance class with Eartha Kitt, this is the definitive American odyssey; and, as he stands in a pigpen with a prize sow, or next to his great-grandfather Cal's gravestone, he is as potent and archetypal an American hero as any in twentieth-century fiction. The most 'poignant' shot of all, with Jimmy standing outside the farmhouse staring in one direction as Markie's dog Tuck stares in the other, Stock saw as Jimmy's interpretation of the Thomas Wolfe title *You Can't Go Home Again*.

As well as the *Life* photo-essay, Jimmy gave other interviews – one of them, with Howard Thompson of the *New York Times*, was even the subject of a Dennis Stock photograph. George Stevens, the director of *Giant*, was later to remark that Jimmy was the only person he knew who could walk into a crowded room and instinctively pick out the four journalists in it. Certainly he had no trouble playing to the press, employing all the tricks – sensitive philosophizing (from *The Little Prince* if not from Plato), establishment-rocking bravado, and apparent candour – at his disposal. 'I'm a serious-minded and intense little devil,' he sighed to the *Los Angeles Times*, 'terrible [sic] gauche

and so tense I don't see how people stay in the same room with me. I know I wouldn't tolerate myself.' His greatest ally in the press became none other than Hedda Hopper, whom he referred to wittily as 'my friend at court'. After seeing *East of Eden*, she was completely won over. When Joe Hyams of the *Herald Tribune* accused him of being phoney with Hedda, Jimmy told him to look at it as 'protective colouration'. 'If I conform to myself, the only one I'm hurting is myself. So instead I'm a nice, polite, well-raised boy full of respect . . .'

Elia Kazan had watched the disease of fame creeping into Jimmy on the set of *East of Eden*. 'When Jimmy was rude to a wardrobe man,' he noted paternally in *A Life*, 'I soon put a stop to that.' In fact, of course, Jimmy was merely assuming the manners of the stardom he had always been grooming himself for. If fame is one of the great diseases of the twentieth century, people do not catch it unwittingly. Jimmy Dean was not, by any stretch of the imagination, an innocent farmboy corrupted by Hollywood. Stardom was his birthright and his mission.

In New York with Stock, Jimmy charged around town basking in anticipation of his glory as the star of *East of Eden*. Once he had been caught by Stock in as many offbeat situations as they could contrive to set up, he left the photographer to amuse himself and hurtled off to spread his good tidings among the 'cattle call' community of actors who hadn't yet enjoyed such strokes of luck. Announcing that he wanted to make a bullfight movie and a biopic about Woody Guthrie, he bought a Bolex 16 mm camera and talked with Roy Schatt about shooting in the studio and garden on East 33rd Street. One night the gang was eating at Schatt's studio when Jimmy picked up a chair and took it out into the middle of the street, proceeding then to sit down and smoke a cigarette as though, Schatt recollected, he were in a gentleman's club. When Schatt and Marty Landau rushed out to find out what all the honking and shouting was about, Jimmy

The drugstore matador at play:
bullfighting, with all its glamour and
flirtation with death, was one of
Jimmy's many pet obsessions

Judging from the bags under his eyes,
a late publicity shot on the set of *Eden*

The curious eternal triangle
of *East of Eden*

Opposite: Like countless young actors
of the time, Jimmy used cigarettes not
merely as drugs but as props

An impromptu guest spot at the
Fairmount High Valentine Dance

A smile for the hometown fans

evening at a party, kissing her goodbye at Grand Central Station and never seeing her again. In an act of callous ingratitude, he refused to lend any money to Rogers Brackett, who had fallen on hard times after being sacked from a job, telling his old friend that he had 'outgrown' him and the Alec Wilder set.

He returned to Hollywood on 8 March, the day before a huge celebrity preview of *East of Eden* at New York's Astor Theatre: a case of 'It's my party and I'll boycott it if I want to.' His absence couldn't have been more conspicuous in the star-studded benefit for the Actors' Studio, where people paid $150 for a ticket and usherettes included Method princesses Marilyn Monroe and Eva Marie Saint. For Jimmy the occasion was too dauntingly dreamlike: better to sabotage it like a sulking child and have people think you're coolly indifferent into the bargain. Reviews of the film veered between the ecstatic and the appalled; certainly none of them was able to feign indifference to Jimmy's Cal Trask. If Bosley Crowther in the *New York Times* deemed his performance a 'mass of histrionic gingerbread' and as slavish an imitation of Brando as it was possible to imagine, many more reviews – including an important one in *Time* magazine on 21 March – recognized that Jimmy was something totally new. Back in Hollywood, where Hedda Hopper raved about the film on 27 March, Elia Kazan witnessed a more telling kind of review when teenagers began screaming for Jimmy during a Hollywood preview. Not since Sinatra's heyday had he seen such hysteria, and years later he confessed that he was 'totally unprepared for Jimmy's success'. By the end of the month, as shooting commenced on *Rebel Without a Cause*, *East of Eden* was the Number 1 grossing film in the country.

'EX-FARMBOY NOW MAKING HAY IN MOVIES', said the *Fairmount News*.

claimed he was merely trying to shake things up a little. Late at night he would hang out at Jerry's Bar on West 54th Street, then drag people back to the little apartment on 68th Street and play his bongoes along to voodoo beat records by Les Baxter. 'I'm playing the damn bongo and the world go to hell,' he would say, grimacing in concentration. Actor Tye Morrow remembers more than a few women ending up in his bed during these weeks, although Jimmy frequently didn't care to perform.

There were two 'for old time's sake' reunions in New York, both with ex-lovers. With Dizzy Sheridan he spent a strained

Adam (Raymond Massey) hears the
bad news about his refrigerated
lettuces from Sheriff Sam Cooper (Burl
Ives)

**Cal in his mother's bordello with Ann
(Lois Smith), the servant-girl**

**Being dragged from his mother's
place. "I just wanna talk to you!"**

CHAPTER FIVE

REBEL

'UNDER ALL THE VIOLENCE AND AGONY JIMMY PROJECTED ON
THE SCREEN, THERE WAS A FUNNY OPTIMISM, A SENSE THAT HE
WOULD COME THROUGH AND BECOME THE GOOD GUY HE
WANTED TO BE.' – STEWART STERN, SCREENPLAY WRITER ON
REBEL WITHOUT A CAUSE

On the set of *Rebel Without a Cause* with Hollywood rebel Nick Ray

Talking through a scene with Ray and Natalie Wood

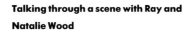

U nlike Elia Kazan, whom he had assisted on *A Tree Grows in Brooklyn* (1944), Nicholas Ray was a newcomer at Warner Brothers. His brief track record included marvellous films like *In a Lonely Place* (1950), *Johnny Guitar* (1954), and, his début, *They Live By Night* (1949), whose doomed lovers Farley Granger and Cathy O'Donnell serve almost as prototypes for Jimmy and Natalie Wood in *Rebel Without a Cause*. Jimmy, mistrustful at the best of times and hankering for a Kazan-style father figure, warmed to his studiedly non-autocratic approach to direction, which encouraged as much input and participation from the juvenile cast as possible. Ray was also a fellow Midwesterner, hailing from Wisconsin.

Screenwriter Leon Uris had turned Nick Ray's story for *Rebel*, 'The Blind Run', into 'the history of an entire community' – a Uris blockbuster approach which Ray felt was thoroughly inappropriate. When ex-schoolteacher Irving Shulman was brought in to replace him, working for three months on a script that outlined the main plot and created the principal characters, he too fell out with Ray. In desperation, the director met with Stewart Stern, a New York friend of Lenny Rosenman's, and gave him a shot at writing a final screenplay from Shulman's adaptation. Credits at the end of the day read: Story:Ray; Adaptation: Shulman; Screenplay: Stern.

Jimmy first met Stewart Stern at the Miller Drive house of the writer's uncle Arthur Loew Jr, grandson of MGM founder Marcus Loew. Determined to outpsych him, Jimmy sat rotating in a swivel chair and blanked him. After several minutes had passed, he suddenly let loose a deafening imitation of a cow, one which had been perfected through years of living on a farm. Much to his surprise, however, Stern replied in kind with an equally convincing 'moo', and before long they had exhausted the entire repertoire of Old MacDonald's Farm. By such circuitous routes did people gain Jimmy's trust. In the planetarium sequence of

High above Hollywood with Jim
Backus, who played Jim Stark's
father in *Rebel*. Backus was more
renowned as the voice of Mr Magoo

Rebel, of course, he used his 'moo' to taunt Buzz and his cronies.

With Stern's screenplay as a base, Jimmy turned the role of Jim Stark into a sustained exercise in angst-ridden improvisation. Jim Backus, the actor (and voice of Mr Magoo) who played Jim's emasculated father in the film, says Jimmy was virtually *Rebel*'s co-director, and even Elia Kazan was astonished by the apparent spontaneity of his protégé's performance. Of Dean's three major film roles, Jim Stark is probably the most

complex and ambivalent, even if by the same token it is the least convincing. Anyone who hadn't seen *Rebel Without a Cause* might assume that its hero was simply a prototype for moody pop youth — such is the iconic stature of the red-jacketed, blue-jeaned image. In fact, Stark is as schizoid and multi-dimensional as Jimmy himself, perpetually wavering between infantilism and adulthood, masculinity and femininity, street cool and suburban sheepishness. As poet Dennis Cooper wrote,

**Signing Natalie Wood's suede
autograph jacket on the set of *Rebel***

**Like Julie Harris in *Eden*, Natalie
Wood was a sister to Jimmy, though
more of an adoring bobby-soxer
than Harris. Like too many of the
people involved in the film she later
died a premature death**

Opposite: Jim Stark at the police station with gang members Goon (Dennis Hopper), Crunch (Frank Mazzola) and Chick (Jack Grinnage)

Below: *Rebel* publicity shot

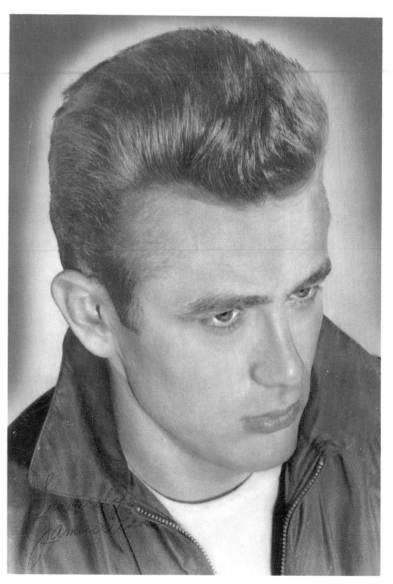

Top: The original half-sheet magazine ad for the film

Bottom: The '70s turned Jimmy into a cliched '50s rock'n'roll icon: this British poster from 1976 says it all

Jimmy's involvement in *Rebel Without a Cause* was such that Jim Backus claimed he virtually co-directed it

Opposite: Jim, Plato and Judy in the temporary sanctuary of the deserted Getty mansion. Stark grows up when he becomes Plato's surrogate daddy for an evening

'his walking-talking plethora of flinches, shrugs and exploding fists represented both his naïveté in matters of the heart and his ambiguity in matters of the crotch ... he was something a slightly more punk Rodin might have brought to life'. While Cal Trask was the most 'twisted, fidgety' kid ever to hit the big screen, Jim Stark — an equally elemental name — verged on psychosis. He is the original middle-class mutant. 'Please lock me up, I'm gonna do something, hit somebody,' he pleads in the Juvenile Hall, but by the end of the film he is playing Mummies and Daddies with Natalie Wood and the doomed, adoring Sal Mineo.

Warner Brothers treated *Rebel Without a Cause* as a glorified B-movie, which, effectively, is what it was. For all the dubious political claims later made for the film by Nick Ray and Dennis Hopper — two of Hollywood's most burnt-out rebels — it wasn't so far removed from the TV psychodramas in which Jimmy had schooled himself in New York. Apart from Jimmy, most of its characters could have waltzed out of a bad script by Clifford Odets, whom Jimmy met at the Chateau Marmont bungalow. If the film is intended as a profound statement about the nihilism of the emerging rock'n'roll generation — the first modern Teenagers — it comes across more as a would-be Cinemascope *West Side Story* without the music. 'We wanted to make our parents over in some magical way,' says Stewart Stern, but so implausible are the dysfunctional parents of *Rebel Without a Cause* that the film's causeless adolescent rebellion seems doubly futile. 'I didn't like the way Nick Ray showed the parents in *Rebel*,' said Elia Kazan, 'but I'd contributed by the way Ray Massey was shown in *Eden*.' 'You gotta do *something*,' says the bullying Buzz when Jim asks him why they are racing the 'blind' chickie run: as *Rebel*'s version of Brando's 'Whaddya got?' it is hardly a satisfactory explanation of the teen malaise in this Californian suburb. Further, Ray overloads the film with metaphysical

116

Between takes with Natalie Wood. Jimmy's red jacket and blue jeans defined a teenage style that influenced a whole generation

Opposite: Sal Mineo adored Jimmy off-camera as much as his character Plato did in the film. Years later, he said, "I understood that I was incredibly in love with him." Mineo was tragically murdered outside his West Hollywood apartment in 1978

Opposite: Stark befriended by Plato on his first day at Dawson High

Below: Stark's hopelessly emasculated father is a curious inversion of the standard patriarchal tyrant

signals – above all, the planetarium professor's dry ruminations on man's cosmic insignificance – but never succeeds in giving them dramatic substance.

'If I just had one day when I didn't feel so confused . . .', says Jim Stark in yet another line that might have been Jimmy himself speaking. When his father, wearing a frilly apron over his suit, tells him that in ten years he will understand what life is about, Jim yells 'I want an answer now!' (Nick Ray said that Jim Stark, like Jimmy himself, was 'seeking an answer, an escape from the surrounding world'.) And yet, as Stewart Stern observed, 'under all the violence and agony Jimmy projected on the screen, there was a funny optimism, a sense that he would come through and become the good boy he wanted to be'. Jim Stark's turning-point comes with the puppy-dog hero worship of little Sal Mineo, whose character, Plato, is just that little bit more unstable than Jimmy's. Through inadvertently parenting the abandoned Plato, Jim awakens to the responsible and loving adult inside himself. In the idyllic pre-Nemesis scene in the empty Getty mansion used for *Sunset Boulevard*, the fugitive trio, Jim, Judy, and Plato, huddle together as father, mother and child. 'Dean's cry of anguish when Mineo is shot down,' noted David Thomson, 'is the very antithesis of the film's inappropriate title.' When Jim is reunited with his parents at the end, the child has become father to the man.

Mineo later admitted that his fascination and idolization of Jimmy was 'sexual to an extent', though at the time he had 'no idea of any understanding of affection between men'. 'It was only years later,' he said, 'that I understood I was incredibly in love with him.' Later still, stabbed to death outside his West Hollywood apartment house, Mineo met the untimely death that he had in common with other people involved with the film: apart from Jimmy himself, Natalie Wood drowned off Catalina Island in 1981, Nick Adams died of a barbiturates overdose in

**Sparring with his friend Perry Lopez
on the set**

**Opposite: Outside the Planetarium at
Griffith Park with Corey Allen, Ian
Wolfe and Sal Mineo**

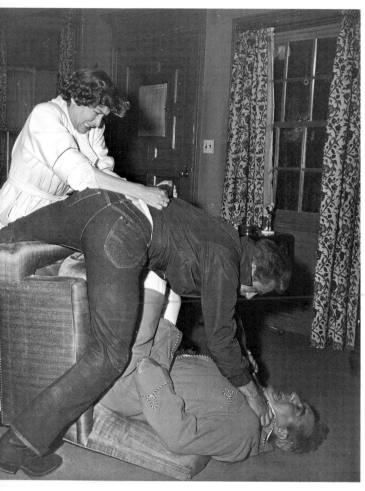

Jim Backus said that Jimmy had "the greatest control over his body of any actor I've ever seen". In this scene he let Jimmy throw him down some stairs, drag him across a room and all but throttle him to death

1968, and Nick Ray died of cancer in 1979. A heavy toll for one film, but, then, some people believe Jimmy's death was itself a jinx.

As in *East of Eden*, Jimmy's performance in the film is made up of a thousand little grimaces, giggles, and quasi-autistic movements. Even more so than in *Eden*, his voice mutters its own kind of disembodied music, coming from so deep within him that it's almost not a part of him. 'He doesn't say much,' gushes Plato to Judy, 'but when he does, you know he means it.' Physically, his body again speaks volumes, especially in the choreography of the switchblade fight with Buzz. 'He had the greatest control over his body of any actor I've ever seen,' wrote Jim Backus in his autobiography *Rocks on the Roof*.

A crucial scene in *Rebel* was where Jim and I had a terrible argument at the top of a staircase, at the climax of which he threw me down the stairs, across the living room, into a chair and tried to choke me to death. I had to put my trust in him. If I for any reason became tense, we both could have been severely injured or even possibly killed. I was 200lb of dead weight, and this boy who couldn't have weighed more that 140 tossed, carried, dragged, and lifted me down those stairs, across the room and into the chair over and over again while they shot their many angles.

Nick Ray was more indulgent with Jimmy than even Elia Kazan had been. Before the long Juvenile Hall sequence at the beginning of the film, Jimmy kept cast and crew waiting an hour while he sat in his dressing-room psyching himself up with wine and Wagner's 'Ride of the Valkyries'. On most other occasions, too, shooting would only commence once he had 'worked himself into his character'. By the end of May, when *Rebel* finished

With boxing coach Mushy Callahan at
Griffith Park

On the beach, probably Malibu, 1955.
Five years earlier Jimmy had felt out
of place here among the golden-
haired surfing bums

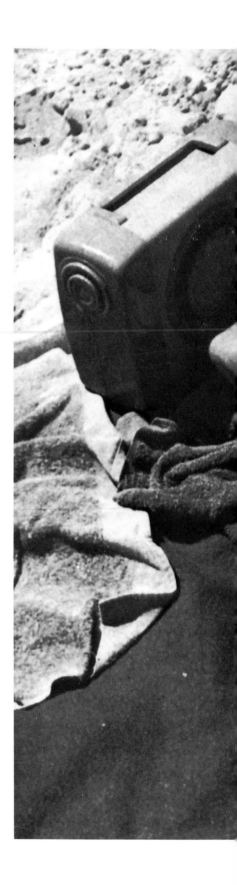

Jimmy often kept cast and crew waiting while he psyched himself up for a scene. Here Nick Ray guides him through a scene in the Juvenile Hall

Opposite: On the set at Griffith Park with Natalie Wood, Nick Ray and Dennis Stock. The latter worked as "dialogue supervisor" on the film

filming, the star and the director were so close that they were even planning their own film project together, provisionally entitled *Heroic Love*. In their synopsis of the film's plot, a young lawyer comes home to a small Western town to study under an attorney he idolizes. When one day he catches the attorney's wife, whom he has himself rejected, *in flagrante delicto* with another man, he says nothing but goes on a spree of seducing the town's women. Subsequently accused by the wife of attempting to seduce her, the young lawyer is horsewhipped out of town. Nothing ever came of the project, but Nick Ray's dissident

anti-Hollywoodism – his refusal to edit *Rebel* was the beginning of a soured relationship with the industry from which he never fully recovered – had made a powerful impression on Jimmy, and it's interesting to speculate whether Jimmy might have ended up playing the same martyred role had he gone into directing. Ray's last years, when he lost an eye in a bar-room fight in Madrid, were spent railing against the system and hoovering up cocaine at Hollywood parties.

But Jimmy was also a huge inspiration to the young company Ray had assembled around him. 'He was incredibly encouraging

**The original middle-class mutant
contemplates the universe**

and sweet,' said Natalie Wood, who remembered him helping her to relax in order to act tense. Dennis Hopper, playing gang member Coon, would take Jimmy aside and ask him what he was doing that made him so different. 'Don't act,' he would counsel. 'If you're smoking a cigarette, smoke it. Don't act like you're smoking it.' Hopper himself rather overdid the Dean 'method' three years later when he fought director Henry Hathaway through 80 takes of a single scene in *From Hell to Texas*.

When the filming of *Rebel* finally ended on 25 May, Jimmy was already rehearsing scenes from *Giant*, the epic melodrama of Texan cattle and oil barons adapted from Edna (*Show Boat*) Ferber's 474-page novel. He had wanted the part of Jett Rink in

George Stevens's film when *Eden* was still being shot, and had inveigled himself into the veteran director's favour by buttering up his assistants. On 17 March, all the brown-nosing paid off when he was officially confirmed for the role of the surly, monosyllabic ranch hand who worships Elizabeth Taylor from afar and thirsts for revenge on her husband Rock Hudson. In the event, it was only Liz Taylor's pregnancy that delayed filming long enough for Jimmy to finish *Rebel Without a Cause* in time. In April he was also confirmed for the role of Rocky Graziano in MGM's *Somebody Up There Likes Me*. Ironically, when the film came, instead, to be made with Paul Newman, Graziano's wife was played by none other than Pier Angeli.

Jim Stark's first day in school

Opposite: Along with Frank Sinatra's Rat Pack, Jimmy was often to be found in Hollywood's Villa Capri restaurant. Here, original Rat Packer Sammy Davis Jr. sniffs out Jimmy's talent as a photographer before introducing him to friends at another table

Looking far from happy on an
agency-arranged film première date
with prototype bimbette Terry Moore

Elizabeth Taylor, shortly to co-star
with him in *Giant*, drops by the set of
Rebel Without a Cause

With Hollywood columnist Sidney
Skolsky at the Villa Capri

**Cracking up with comedian Milton
Berle at the Villa Capri**

Playing outdoor chess with Perry
Lopez

Opposite: Signing autographs on the
set of *Rebel*

With Pat Hardy in *The Unlighted Road*, a CBS *Schlitz Playhouse* production in May 1955

On 6 May, just after completing *Rebel's* night scenes at the Griffith Park Planetarium, Jimmy appeared on CBS's *Schlitz Playhouse* in a teleplay called 'The Unlighted Road'. In what was his last TV role, he netted a cool $2500, playing a young drifter, Jeff Latham, who is unwittingly involved in racketeering and murder. Set up by two older men in a backroads diner, he eventually goes to the police to confess what has happened, only to be released and reunited with his girlfriend played by Pat Hardy.

Joe Hyams, whose house Jimmy would often visit bringing ice cream for Hyams's five-year-old son Jay, says *Rebel Without a Cause* had become as much a substitute universe for Jimmy as *East of Eden* had been. Completely immersed in the role of Jim Stark, he spent less time going on what Bill Bast called the 'Stanislavskian explorations' of the 'Night Watch', and less time chasing cars and women. But cars and women remained important: shortly before *Rebel* had started shooting, he'd bought a $4000 white Porsche Speedster in Hollywood and

On the set of *The Unlighted Road* with
Pat Hardy

As the ingenuous drifter Jeff Latham
in *The Unlighted Road*

driven with Swedish actress Lili Kardell to race in Palm Springs. 'He made no bones about it with the studio executives that racing interested him far more than acting,' wrote Dennis Stock, who worked as a 'dialogue supervisor' on *Rebel*, 'and this was an affront to their corporate and creative dignity.' 'Racing is the only time I feel whole,' Jimmy told an interviewer before proceeding to win the first day's amateur race and come in third in the professional race the following day. Needless to say, the producers of *Rebel Without a Cause* were unhappy about Jimmy risking his life on the racetrack, and got an assurance from him that he wouldn't race during the making of the film.

Apart from Lili Kardell, several women passed in and out of Jimmy's life after Pier Angeli's marriage. With Lew Bracker, a fellow racing aficionado, he chased women in bars and at parties, and when his old pal Whitey Rust visited from Indiana a week of hellraising and reckless driving around Hollywood ensued. One of Jimmy's favoured seduction techniques was to take girls home and play his famous bullfighting game: as he dropped his cape and plunged in for the 'kill', he would simultaneously drop his pants. More reliable, however, was the straightforward appeal to

At Palm Springs before racing the
Speedster

Opposite: Jimmy in the white Porsche
Speedster he bought in Hollywood
for $4000

With his tempestuous girlfriend
Ursula Andress at the Villa Capri,
August 1955

a woman's maternal instincts, wherein he would simply curl up with his head on her lap. 'All women want to mother you,' he told Joe Hyams, adding that he was more successful with older women and that he'd even had an affair with a teacher at college. Marilyn Morrison, ex-wife of singer Johnnie Ray, was one of the 'older women', as was 43-year-old Barbara Hutton, the alcoholic Woolworth's heiress who picked him up one insomniac night at Googie's and took him back to her cottage at the Beverly Hills Hotel.

His one major affair after Pier was with another young European actress, Ursula Andress — later to find fame rising Venus-like from the sea in the first James Bond film *Dr No*.

With Andress at the first Thalians
dinner, 1955

Composer Lenny Rosenman was
struck by how much Andress
resembled Jimmy, and believed the
relationship was essentially
narcissistic for both of them

The manic little-boy laugh which featured so prominently in *Rebel*

Opposite: Jimmy had to try his hand at everything. Photography was something he'd started dabbling in during his New York days

Having spotted her at a Hollywood party, he asked Joe Hyams to 'make me a big man with her' and help him get some publicity for her. When he finally won her over, the affair was tempestuous and obsessive. Bill Bast remembers Andress's European disdain for his Hollywood phoniness, while Lenny Rosenman says the relationship was essentially narcissistic for both of them: as with Mick and Bianca, or Prince and Vanity, the physical resemblance was too striking to be coincidental. (The Amazonian Andress described herself as 'the female Brando'.) Vampira, who had reason to be jealous, recalls that Jimmy had little respect for Andress, and felt that he was 'using her for physical reasons — she was the voluptuous pin-up lady'.

Friends like Bill, Lenny, and Vampira were beginning to fall out with Jimmy at this time. Lenny tired of his snobbery towards Hollywood – 'Really he loved it,' he says, 'because in Hollywood he could believe he was an intellectual' – and, more importantly, felt the boy was deeply disturbed. With several other friends and colleagues he persuaded Jimmy to see an analyst. 'I think he was still in analysis at the time of his death,' he says. As for Bill and Vampira, they merely felt discarded on the wayside of Jimmy's ruthless path to stardom.

Jimmy as moody male model: this portrait could have come from any fashion magazine in the '80s

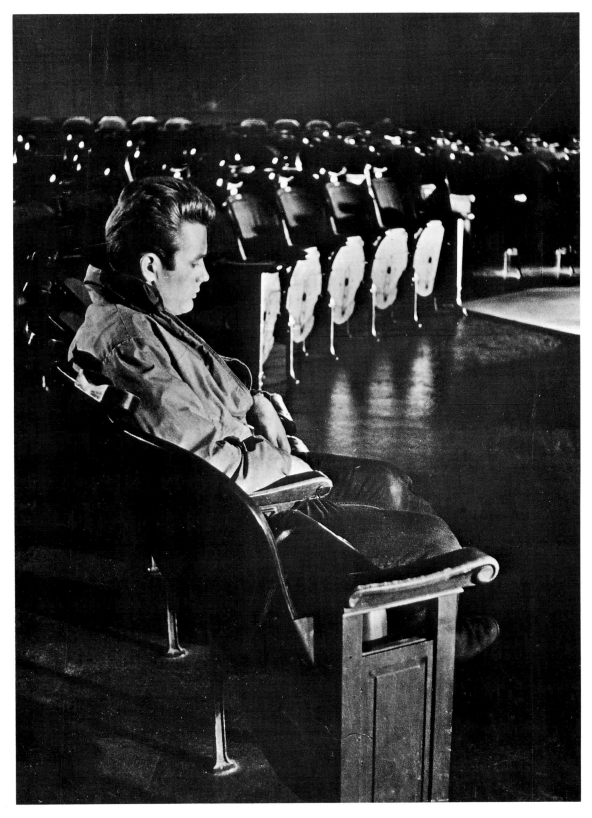

Jim Stark alone in the planetarium. "A star, increasingly bright and increasingly near..."

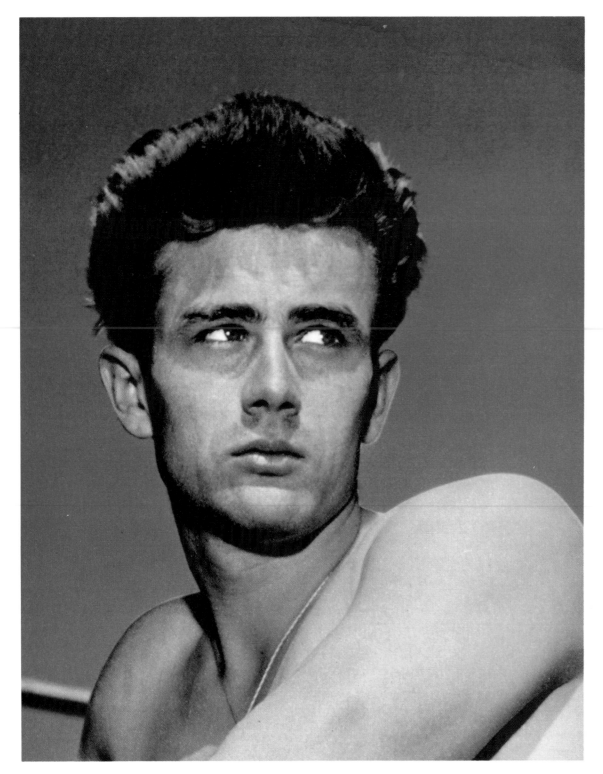

The new star rising, 1954

Jimmy with some of the trophies he'd
won in his Porsche

Jimmy as wasted rock'n'roll casualty.
The statuette is a Foreign Press
Award for his role in *East of Eden*

Opposite: On his motorbike at
Burbank

CHAPTER SIX

GIANT

'HE WAS THE RUNT IN A LITTER OF THOROUGHBREDS, AND YOU
COULD FEEL THE LONELINESS BEATING OUT OF HIM.'
MERCEDES McCAMBRIDGE, LUZ BENEDICT IN *GIANT*

If *East of Eden* was a big-budget, Cinemascope art film and *Rebel Without a Cause* a jumped-up B-movie, then George Stevens's *Giant* was the only true Hollywood 'production' to feature James Dean. Unlike Elia Kazan or Nick Ray, Stevens was no rebel maverick: he hailed from an earlier generation of directors and by the mid-1950s was undisputed King Of The Epic. 'The concentric classicism of the Stevens frame,' wrote American critic Andrew Sarris, 'almost looked like an official style for national epics.' To Jimmy he was like a John Ford or a Howard Hawks, a pantheon director one

fought to work with. Little did the new star, given equal billing with Liz Taylor and Rock Hudson, realize how incompatible his approach to acting was going to be.

Adapted by Fred Guiol and Ivan Moffat, Edna Ferber's novel was based partly on the career of Glen McCarthy, a rags-to-stinking-riches Houston oilman who served as the model for Jimmy's character, Jett Rink. If the film today looks rather like a three-hour 1950s pilot for *Dallas*, for its director it formed the third part of an 'American Dream' trilogy with the similarly epic *A Place in the Sun* (1951) and *Shane* (1953). Jett Rink

A Belgian poster for *Giant*, 1957

Opposite: A day at the races

Another eternal triangle for Jimmy: with Elizabeth Taylor (Leslie) and Rock Hudson (Bick) in a publicity still

symbolized the ultimate perversion of that dream, offering Jimmy the chance to complete his own trilogy playing an all-American anti-hero, a rock'n'roll cowboy who ends his life as an alcoholic tycoon in a tuxedo. As in the Manichean psychodrama of *Eden*, Dean is posited as the dark, remote, sexually disturbing counterpoint to a sturdy, honest rival, in this case Rock Hudson (playing Bick Benedict). The fact that in real life Jimmy felt as hostile to Hudson as Rink does to Benedict only helped matters.

Filming had started on *Giant* at the end of May, with location shooting in Virginia that didn't feature Jimmy. The weekend before joining the production on 3 June, he entered his Porsche in a Memorial Day race at Santa Barbara, but had to pull off the track when his engine blew. Subsequently barred from all driving competitions by George Stevens, it turned out to be his last race. On his return to Hollywood, he immediately began preparing for his role by mugging up on Texan history and cattle-raising. The cowboy clothes suited him fine: what more romantic image of lone-ranging masculinity can you get than Levi's, cowboy boots, and a ten-gallon hat? True to his total involvement in his characters he rarely changed out of this get-up, and by the time the 280-strong company descended on Marfa, Texas, at the beginning of a boiling July, he had perfected a Texan accent, taught himself to rope cattle, and was hunting jack rabbits at night. 'Jimmy was a dedicated perfectionist actor,' wrote Mercedes McCambridge, who played Rock Hudson's sister, Luz Benedict, in the film. 'I watched him develop bits of business until they seemed a part of his nature. He asked cowboys to teach him intricate tricks with a rope. He worked himself bleary-eyed with that rope, but if you watch him as Jett Rink doing tricks with it, you will see a Texas boy who has been working with a rope all his cotton-pickin' life!'

Marfa was 59 miles from the Mexican border and a

Rock'n' roll cowboy in a ten-gallon hat, Marfa, Texas

On the set of *Giant* back in Hollywood

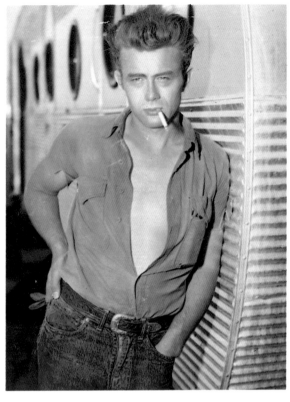

A definitively cool pose in Texas

**Liz Taylor drops in to see Jett at 'Little
Reata', where he will shortly strike oil**

163

Jimmy liked horses almost as much as he liked cars and motorbikes. Perhaps this one in Marfa reminded him of the Palomino he kept in Santa Barbara

Opposite: Jimmy and Rock Hudson despised each other as much as their respective characters did. Hudson found Jimmy's acting nerve-rackingly unpredictable

three-and-a-half-hour drive from El Paso. Exactly as it appears in the film, it was slap-bang in the middle of nowhere, a desert town of under 3000 people where a severe drought had lasted for over five years. Here Stevens built the $200,000 Gothic mansion which rises so surrealistically from the flat landscape – an extravagant prop used solely for exterior shots in the film and left behind to stand as a bizarre monument until it crumbled to the ground in the early 1980s – and here began the bitter clash between his benevolent directorial despotism and Jimmy Dean's radically dissident approach to acting. 'The more Jimmy became aware of the mechanics of Stevens's approach,' wrote Bill Bast, 'the more he began resenting the man.' Alfred Hitchcock said actors were cattle, but Stevens appeared consciously to treat them as such; perhaps he confused them with the thousands of cattle actually featured in the film. What Andrew Sarris called

his 'concentric classicism' was simply the result of shooting scenes from every conceivable angle and then spending months editing out miles of excess footage. Jimmy despised it, and quickly distanced himself from both cast and crew. Only Dennis Hopper, who'd come on from *Rebel Without a Cause* and with whom Jimmy would often smoke pot off the set, proved an ally among the men in the film. Otherwise Jimmy was forced to rely on all the little-boy-lost charm he could muster to gain sympathy from the women. 'I can't tell you how he wanted to be patted,' wrote Mercedes McCambridge. 'He was the runt in a litter of thoroughbreds, and you could feel the loneliness beating out of him.'

Jane Withers, who played the curiously-named Vashti Snythe, became another of Jimmy's mother-surrogates, while even Elizabeth Taylor, after some preliminary mind-games on

Jimmy's part, became a big sister — and an ally against Stevens, since she had her own problems with the director. Gossip-mongers hinted at romance, but the friendship was not unlike the one she had had with that other sexually ambiguous actor, Montgomery Clift, in Stevens's earlier *A Place in the Sun*. (Jimmy was so nervous in his first scene with Taylor, however that to loosen up he marched off and peed in front of hundreds of spectators who'd gathered around Stevens's 'open' set.)

Raymond Massey had found Jimmy's improvisations exasperating in *East of Eden*. In *Giant* the director himself had no patience with the liberties Jimmy attempted to take with the script, nipping in the bud any spontaneous touches he tried to add to his part. It's a wonder that so much of Jimmy survives in the film, even if — ironically — the most distinctive things about his performance are the gestures of closing off from the other characters: mumbling into his chest, pulling the brim of his Stetson down over his eyes. Ultimately, his Jett Rink is a study in loneliness; this is a Cal Trask grown up with no proper niche in society and no place to call home — until he inherits the tiny tract of land that turns into a monstrous billion-dollar oilfield. And, like Orson Welles's Citizen Kane, another ageing tycoon played by a 24-year-old, he ends his life pitifully alone.

Another ally on the set, and Jimmy's last photographic Boswell, was Sanford Roth, who had been sent down to Texas to do a photo-essay on Jimmy for *Collier's* magazine. Roth immediately scored highly in Jimmy's estimation because he had lived in Europe and photographed such illustrious figures as Picasso, Braque, Chagall, Leger, Einstein, Cocteau and Stravinsky. On returning to Hollywood, the 49-year-old photographer and his wife Beulah became that impossible thing for Jimmy: a mom and pop with intellectual credibility. They adopted him, took pictures of him, and encouraged him in intellectual and artistic pursuits. 'He wanted to walk down the Boulevard

Jimmy confronts Jett Rink's destiny

Inspecting the *Dallas*-style models of
Jetoil wells with *Giant* writers Fred
Guiol and Ivan Moffat

Opposite: Looking over set designs
with Fred Guiol

Laughing with Ivan Moffat

Montparnasse,' remembered Roth, who died in Rome in 1962; 'he wanted to study sculpture in Paris, buy crazy sweaters in Capri, and meet Cocteau and Miro.' Sitting in their house with their cat Louis on his lap, Jimmy would read Curcio Malaparte and Genet's *Thief's Journal* and talk of seeing Europe before the year was out. 'I was never sure whether his interest in writers like Genet was intellectual pretense or really valid,' wrote Beulah Roth some years later, 'but he did renounce Edgar Guest in their favour.' When one day he decided that acting wasn't a truly creative medium, he badgered Roth into introducing him to sculptress Pegot Waring, who accepted him as a student. Down in Texas, Roth took some brilliant shots of Jimmy, most of them involving ropes: practising his lassoing technique with some Mexican extras, tying up Liz Taylor in some innocently sexual horseplay, playing hanged man with a noose round his neck like the one he later kept in his Sherman Oaks apartment. They are among the sexiest pictures ever taken of him.

When the *Giant* company returned to Burbank at the end of July, Jimmy's relations with Stevens deteriorated even further. Now that he was back in the swing of Hollywood nightlife again, usually in the company of the hot-tempered Ursula Andress, he often rolled up late at the studio, and one day he didn't roll up at all. Claiming Stevens had kept him waiting around on the set to no purpose the day before, he decided to play truant and spend a day moving into the Sherman Oaks apartment he was renting from Nico Romanos, maitre d' at his favourite restaurant and hangout, the Villa Capri. Unfortunately, after Mercedes McCambridge had slipped and fallen in her shower that morning, Jimmy was required on set, and no one could find him. The next day Stevens exploded at Jimmy in front of the entire cast and crew, and Hollywood was soon buzzing with news of the dressing-down. Among many gossipers, most of them gloating at the Wunderkind's come-uppance, only Hedda Hopper came to his

The affair with Ursula Andress came to a stormy end not long after *Giant's* cast and crew returned to Hollywood

Bondage games with Liz and Big Rock

Liz lassoes George Stevens while Mercedes McCambridge (Luz), Rock and Jimmy look on

rescue, deeming it 'high time we had a talk'. 'George Stevens is a martinet, a slow-moving hulk of a man who tried to force Jimmy to conform to his interpretation,' she wrote before recounting how she explained to Jimmy that producer Henry Ginsberg would lose millions if anything sabotaged the production at this stage. 'Jimmy Dean has been clobbered by some of the Hollywood press,' she concluded.

'but I've gotta go along with Jimmy. After being called to work day after day and doing nothing more than sit around while Rock Hudson played love scenes with Elizabeth Taylor, Dean got bored stiff and just didn't show the next time he was called. Frankly, he felt he wasn't getting a fair shake from those in command, and when the higher-ups took the attitude that Dean would do what they said or else, they made a mistake. Jimmy called a bluff. A highly emotional guy, he likes to be wanted, and some people with this picture treated him like a dog. Silly attitude.'

Designed like a hunting lodge, the Sherman Oaks apartment at 14611 Sutton Street became the Hollywood equivalent of Jimmy's pad in New York. Full of bizarre objects like a huge bronze eagle, a white bearskin rug, and the hangman's noose – together with two tape machines, a 16mm Bolex movie camera, an easel, and the usual quota of bongoes – it was a place to entertain friends and intriguing strangers alike, and music often blared out of the little house late into the night. As did the sound of arguments with Ursula Andress: on 12 August the *Hollywood Reporter* noted that Jimmy was learning German 'so that he can fight with Ursula Andress in two languages'. Only when Liz Taylor, seeing how much he loved Sanford and Beulah Roth's cat Louis, bought Jimmy a Siamese kitten did the noise simmer

Jimmy in his Sherman Oaks apartment, deeply absorbed in the *Hollywood Reporter*

Pocket chess with a small feathered friend

Jimmy at home, listening to tapes

Opposite: "I'm playing the damn
bongo and the world go to hell..."

Jett at home, showing Mrs Benedict around

Opposite: Tea for Mrs Benedict. Jett worships her but never betrays his feelings

down a little. Jimmy named him Marcus.

As with Cal Trask and Jim Stark, the role of Jett Rink — another two-syllable, ever-so-slightly-improbable name — drew on so much of Jimmy's personality that the question how good a performance seems almost immaterial. From our very first sight of him, with the ever-present Chesterfield in the corner of his mouth and looking like some apprentice Clint Eastwood, he is the Jimmy Dean who simultaneously pushes people away and wants boyishly to be loved by them. With Liz Taylor he is instinctively the same awkward, seemingly bashful boy he is with

Julie Harris and Natalie Wood in his previous films. Most touchingly, when Liz drops in on him at his property, 'Little Reata', his shack not only has a newspaper picture of her on the wall but shows exactly the same signs of earnest self-improvement that characterized Jimmy's life — even the booklet on 'How To Speak And Write Masterly English' is not so far from his desperate desire to improve his mind. (In fact, writing was probably Jimmy's biggest hang-up; for all his success as an actor, he felt he would only ever be somebody if he could write.) Jimmy has never been more vulnerable and lovable than in this

The ageing tycoon takes a drunken swing at Bick

scene, and inevitably it's a vulnerability – and an innocence – which is lost the second he strikes oil and stands doused in black liquid like some primal avenging swamp creature. As the ageing tycoon, rotting with alcohol and resentment, he is considerably more convincing than either Hudson or Taylor, who appear to change with the passing years only insofar as their hair turns blue. Like Brando's Don Corleone crossed with a sleazy Clark Gable, he conjures a figure at once pathetic and strangely glamorous. Is this perhaps how Jimmy himself might have ended up?

George Stevens's principal objection to Jimmy was that he couldn't accept being a mere part of the story of *Giant*: accustomed by now to being the central protagonist of the drama, he saw the film exclusively from Jett Rink's view – which, given the numbingly one-dimensional characters around him, was hardly surprising. In Stevens's epic scheme of things, he himself – the invisible *auteur*ist deity – was the real star, his panoramic overview the only possible vision.

As filming neared completion at the beginning of September, Jimmy finally resigned himself to being a mere ingredient in the master chef's recipe. 'There really isn't an opportunity for greatness in this world,' he wrote with typical pomposity to the Rev. James DeWeerd. 'We are impaled on a crock of conditioning. A fish that is in water has no choice that he is. Genius would have it that he swim in sand ... we are fish and we drown.' In August he announced that he hoped to form his own production company within Warner Brothers, including, among possible film projects, *The Little Prince*, the story of Billy The Kid, and a ballet based on Bartok's *The Miraculous Mandarin*. Meanwhile, Jane Deacy lined up two major TV roles for him in New York, Morgan Evans in an NBC production of Emlyn Williams's *The Corn Is Green* (the fee a cool $20,000) and a part in an adaptation of Hemingway's story 'The Battler', to be directed by

Jimmy recovers from his crude-oil
shower

With Sarita Monteill on the _Giant_ set at Burbank

didn't let go of her with much grace or dignity, pursuing her around Hollywood on his motorbike and storming into a restaurant where she was eating with Derek. Consolation was found in the attentions of yet another European actress, Leslie Caron, whom he squired around town while on the rebound. 'Foreign girls intrigue me,' he confessed to one gossip writer. Perhaps their apparent unattainability, their distance from ordinary apple-pie American womanhood, made them the more enticing proposition. After Jimmy's death it was widely reported that Ursula Andress wept hysterically on hearing the news and blamed her termination of the affair for it.

On the Burbank set of _Giant_, Jimmy met two old Hollywood heroes, Gary Cooper and Humphrey Bogart. Bogart especially meant a lot to him, and when Joe Hyams brought him along one day, Jimmy was tongue-tied with awe: 'literally', Hyams later wrote. 'He sat at Bogart's feet mumbling pleasantries and agreeing with everything the older star said.' Bogart had seen something of his own rebellion in Brando and Jimmy, but left unconvinced by the latter, subsequently telling the press that if Jimmy had lived 'he'd never have been able to live up to his publicity'. For his part, Jimmy came away from the encounter more certain than ever that he had nothing to do with the old-guard celluloid heroes. 'Bogie and Cooper and Gable,' Hyams reported him as saying as they drove away from the studio, 'they're different to me. No matter what the role, they're always themselves because they have such strong personalities.' It's a measure of his inner uncertainties that he didn't think of _himself_ as a strong personality, but then the particular point about Jimmy is that his strength is in the very search _for_ personality — the adolescent's struggle for self-definition. As Bogart remarked to Hyams, Jimmy was 'too conscious of himself every minute' to project the kind of macho authority Hollywood expected of its heroes.

a young Arthur Penn. (Penn was not long afterwards to direct Paul Newman as Billy The Kid in _The Left-Handed Gun_.) In early September, Deacy flew to Hollywood to renegotiate Jimmy's contract and to find him a professional business management team. With Dick Clayton she approached the firm of Carl Coultree and William Gray, who agreed to take him on as a client.

A blow to Jimmy's pride came when Ursula Andress ditched him for John Derek, rising young heart-throb and future husband of Bo. Maila Nurmi (Vampira) remembers that he

Jimmy had been ruthless with Rogers Brackett in New York, but he showed his generosity when Bill Bast tried to break out of the rut of sit-com writing that he'd fallen into in Hollywood. Apart from treating him to meals at the Villa Capri and bringing him round to the Roths' house, on the very last occasion they met he lent him money so that he could write the 'serious' TV script he'd been planning for months. Bill later ended up writing episodes of *The Waltons* and *The Colbys*, but not for want of his friend's help – though Jimmy doubtless owed it anyway from the days in the Santa Monica penthouse.

It's a fine irony that virtually the last job Jimmy did before his death was a short film interview for the National Highway Committee extolling the virtues of safe driving. Shuffling awkwardly in his seat in the obligatory Stetson and jeans, he tells interviewer Gig Young: 'I use-ta fly around quite a bit. Took a lot of unnecessary chances on the highway. Now I drive extra cautious.' As he gets up to leave, Young asks him if he has anything else he wants to say, to which Jimmy replies: 'Take it easy driving, because the life you might save might be ... *mine*.' The whole thing has the effect of, say, Keith Richards warning teenagers against drugs.

At this very time, moreover, Jimmy was hanging out at every available opportunity with the German mechanics at Competition Motors on North Vine Street, having made a down-payment on a new $6900 Porsche 550 Spyder, a far more serious racing car than the earlier Speedster. Planning to enter a race in Salinas, between LA and San Francisco, the moment *Giant* had finished shooting, he wanted the car – with its top speed of 170 mph – ready and raring to go. Horst Rieschel, Tony Buechler, and Rolf Wuetherich were the three mechanics who'd been brought over from Germany to work in Hollywood, and Jimmy had made it a condition of sale that one of them, Wuetherich, accompany him to every race the car was entered for. The deal

Charming *Giant* authoress Edna Ferber on the set

finally went through on 21 September.

On 23 September 1955, when Jimmy met Alec Guinness at the Villa Capri and took him outside to see the car, the English actor warned him that he could break his neck in it. The next day, George Stevens finished filming the banquet scene at the end of *Giant*, with Jimmy mumbling incoherently into the microphone in a curious parody of the Last Supper. At last the film, with its backstage battles worthy of Truffaut's *Day for Night*, was behind him, and Jimmy was free to run wild for a week before the race at the weekend and the projected return to

Jimmy at the wheel of the
Porsche 550 Spyder in which he was
to die, 30 September 1955. It cost him
$6900

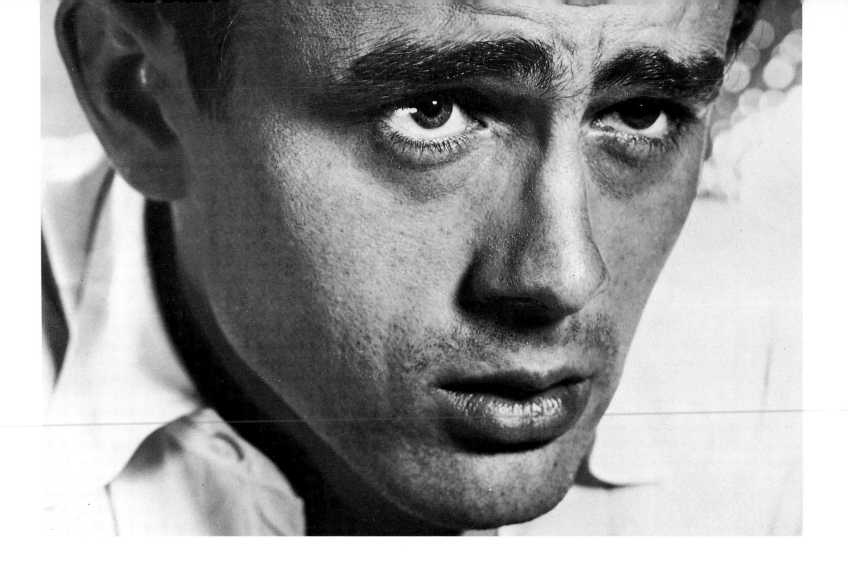

New York for *The Corn is Green*. Things couldn't have been looking much better for him: Jane Deacy had had his Warners contract upped to a $100,000 advance per film, and *Rebel Without a Cause* was due to open across America within a month. Jimmy even started to think ahead for once, talking with his racing pal Lew Bracker about a life insurance policy. (In the event, though it was drawn up by Bracker, it was never signed.)

Jimmy wanted company on the drive up to Salinas, and tried to persuade various members of his family to come with him. Staying with his father that week were Marcus and Ortense Winslow and Jimmy's uncle Charlie Nolan Dean, all of whom had driven from Indiana for a family reunion. None of them could come, however, and by the middle of the week it looked as though only Wuetherich and Bill Hickman, Jimmy's dialogue

coach and jack-rabbit-hunting companion on *Giant*, would be going with him. At the last minute, however, Sandy Roth – who had said he couldn't make it because of his deadline for the *Collier's* photo-essay on Jimmy – agreed to come. Adding to the irony of Jimmy's highway safety film, he said pictures of Jimmy racing would make a good conclusion to the article.

On Thursday, 29 September, Jimmy dropped by the apartment of a girl he was seeing, Jeanette Miller, and left the kitten Marcus with her. That night, as he often did before racing, he deserted his friends and disappeared. Later it was learned that he's gone to a gay party at Malibu Colony, leaving when one of his gay friends demanded that he come out of the closet and stop leading a double life. Early the next morning he drove to Competition

Motors to give the Spyder a final inspection with Rolf Wueth-erich, then had a late breakfast with his father and his uncle Charlie. Around lunchtime, he and Rolf picked up Bill Hickman and Sandy Roth and decided they would drive up the coast in the Spyder while Bill and Sandy followed in Jimmy's Ford station wagon. Not long before Bakersfield, Jimmy gave his last autograph when he signed a speeding ticket given him by patrolman Otie Hunter. Seventeen miles north of the city he turned west on to Highway 466, the landscape becoming increasingly dry and barren, and stopped shortly after 5 p.m. to chat with Lance Reventlow, the 21-year-old son of his one-night-stand heiress Barbara Hutton. Reventlow was also entered for the Salinas race, driving a 300 SL Mercedes.

With the sun going down just before 5.45 p.m., 23-year-old Donald Turnupseed, an engineering student driving from San Luis Obispo to Tulare in a 1950 Ford Tudor, couldn't see the silver Spyder as he pulled into its path off the Y-shaped intersection of Highways 466 and 41. Bill Hickman had already warned Jimmy that the Porsche was becoming dangerously inconspicuous on the road. Whether Jimmy was wearing his glasses or not no one to this day can be sure. Although he is said to have heard him say 'That guy's got to see us' — Jimmy's last words — Rolf Wuetherich was in a semi-doze in the passenger seat and hadn't noticed whether Jimmy had the glasses on.

Exactly who saw what and who misjudged which distance remains a matter of contention among Dean buffs to this day, as the recent publication of Warren Newton Beath's bizarre *Death of James Dean* makes only too clear. The facts are that Jimmy careered into the side of the far sturdier Ford, sustained fatal injuries immediately, and died within minutes. Turnupseed was almost unhurt. Wuetherich, thrown out of the Spyder on impact, lived to tell the tale (to *Modern Screen*) and sue the James Dean estate for $100,000. Two patrolmen and an ambulance were on the scene within 15 minutes. And Sandy Roth, a faithful Boswell to the last, took pictures of Jimmy's shattered body that have never been seen. An actor was dead and a twentieth-century legend was born.

That night in Hollywood, young actors and actresses wept outside Googie's. Jimmy's was the third premature death to hit the film industry in as many months — Suzan Ball and Robert (*Caine Mutiny*) Francis had also recently died in accidents — but the new breed of Method-inspired actors were particularly shocked by his loss. More even than Brando, Jimmy Dean had inadvertently opened doors to actors who ten years earlier would never have made it in Hollywood — boys who weren't classically handsome heroes, girls who weren't goddesses. Like a revolutionary leader, he was an inspiration to a generation. Even Tab Hunter, an uncomplicated pretty boy if ever there was one, maintained that Jimmy's oddball personality and lifestyle were seminal influences on the cultural upheavals to come in the 1960s. If Nick Ray and Dennis Hopper over-dramatized his importance as 'the first student activist' and 'the first guerrilla artist to work in movies', there is still some truth in the well-worn statement that if Brando changed the way people acted, Jimmy changed the way they lived. Elvis Presley, who translated Jimmy's revolution into the founding moments of rock'n'roll, was as infatuated with him as Jimmy was with Brando, and learned the script of *Rebel Without a Cause* virtually by heart. Not long afterwards, in Hibbing, Minnesota — it could as easily have been Fairmount, Indiana — scrawny young Robert Zimmerman, later Bob Dylan, re-invented himself as the town's very own proto-punk in Dean jeans and Brando leather: just another Midwestern misfit limbering up for superstardom.

On the set of *Giant*, wrapping up final scenes, Elizabeth Taylor heard the news and collapsed; shooting was postponed as she recovered in hospital, and a year later she refused to attend

closest boyhood pals, were the six pallbearers. It was a huge affair, the biggest public gathering the town had ever seen and the beginning of the cult worship of Jimmy which has continued for almost 35 years.

Steve Brooks and the rest of the Warners publicity machine could hardly fail to see the potential in releasing *Rebel Without a Cause* the week after Jimmy's death; a black humourist might suggest that dying was the best career move he ever made. If reviewers were less than complimentary about the film itself, few could resist the pathos of watching Jimmy dice with death onscreen yet emerge like a phoenix from the ashes of his teen torment. In France, François Truffaut, still a young critic on *Cahiers du Cinema*, saw that Jimmy was far more than a middle-class delinquent.

'In James Dean' [he wrote], 'today's youth discovers itself. Less for the reasons usually advanced – violence, sadism, hysteria, pessimism, cruelty and filth – than for others infinitely more simple and commonplace: modesty of feeling, continual fantasy life, moral purity without relation to everyday morality but all the more rigorous, eternal adolescent love of tests and trials, intoxication, pride, and regret at feeling oneself "outside" society, refusal and desire to become integrated and, finally, acceptance – or refusal – of the world as it is.'

the Academy awards when they declined to honour Jimmy with a posthumous Oscar. Marcus and Ortense Winslow only heard the awful news after the long journey home to Fairmount. Winton Dean took his son's body back to Indiana on the Tuesday and set the funeral for the following Saturday. For three days it was kept at Hunt's Funeral Home, then taken on the Saturday to the Friends' Church.

Among the 3000 mourners were *Giant* producer Henry Ginsberg, Warners publicity man Steve Brooks, Lew Bracker and Dennis Stock; few others from Hollywood bothered to make the trip. The service was taken by Xan Harvey, pastor at the church, and by James DeWeerd, then pastor at the Cable Tabernacle in Indianapolis, who – ever eccentric and now rather flamboyant as well – flew into Fairmount by private plane after a revival telecast in Cincinnati. Whitey Rust, Paul Smith, Robert Pulley, Robert Middleton, James Faulkerson and Rex Bright, his

In due course, *Rebel* made Warners millions and sparked off a series of even more transparently 'B'-quality movies about juveniles: two of them, *Crime in the Streets* and *Rock, Pretty Baby* (both 1956), even starred Sal Mineo, while *Juvenile Jungle* (1958) boasted Corey Allen (Buzz in *Rebel*). Others included *Hot Rod Girl* (1956), *Untamed Youth* (1957), *Dragstrip Girl* (1957),

Hot Car Girl (1958), and *Dragstrip Riot* (1958). In Europe, *Die Halbstarken* (1956) – 'The Half-Strong' – starred a Teutonic version of Jimmy called Horst Bucholtz, while in Poland Andrzej Wajda's classic *Ashes and Diamonds* (1958) featured the far more interesting Zbigniew Cybulski, himself to die prematurely nine years later. 'I just felt I wanted to be James Dean,' said a typical English fan of the time. 'He made a cock-up of everything, but somehow he seemed to say it all.'

Coupled with the effect of his death, *Rebel Without a Cause* made Jimmy the eternal Youth of cinema, an angst-ridden Peter Pan who never ages but lives on in imagery and celluloid dreams. When Bill Bast later visited his old room-mate's grave, he drove past a sign saying 'Fairmount – Birthplace of James Dean' and realized that 'they were going to take my friend and turn him into something I would never recognize again'. Take him they did, processing him through myriad memorabilia, moulding him into a thousand badges, life masks, T-shirts, and sculptures. Two pulp novels based on his life were ex-Warners publicity man Walter Ross's *The Immortal* (1958), about Midwest foster child Johnny Preston, and Edwin Corley's *Farewell, My Slightly Tarnished Hero* (1971), whose John Calvin Lewis not only appears in the films *Paradise Gate*, *Chicken Run*, and *Texas*, but also picks up transvestite Dick Davine at a Hollywood New Year's Eve party.

By July 1956, four months before *Giant* was released, Warner Brothers were receiving 7000 letters a month from all over the world, all of them addressed to Jimmy. An eerie phenomenon was developing, whose sole precedent was the death of Rudolph Valentino in the 1920s. George Stevens even received letters threatening his life if he cut a single frame of Jimmy out of *Giant*. 'This ruthless, selfish, egotistical young fool was nobody's idol until our children were told that he was,' huffed Ben (*Dragnet*) Alexander in 1958, but girls and boys alike had found something in Jimmy's screen performances that meant more than the transitory sex appeal of matinée idols. 'It wasn't so much the rebelliousness,' says a female fan quoted in David Dalton's *American Icon*. 'We could rebel. It was the vulnerability which we couldn't show, which we didn't dare show because we were fighting it so hard.' Twenty-five years after his death, in 1980, the power of this vulnerability could still be gauged by the 1000 or so fans who congregated at the side of his gravestone to listen to Martin Sheen pay tribute to him. (Sheen, Richard Gere, and Matt Dillon represent three generations of Hollywood actors directly influenced by Jimmy.)

'Live fast, die young, and have a good-looking corpse,' says one of the characters in Nick Ray's *Knock on Any Door* (1949). It's a famous line now, and Jimmy loved to quote it then, but to suppose that he really lived in the spirit of its sentiment would be a mistake. Certainly he flirted with death and loved to alarm people by brushing against it, but his darker side was not a suicidal one and he did not want to die on Highway 466 that Friday afternoon. When Jimmy said death was the only thing he respected, he was probably just quoting a half-remembered line from Rimbaud.

I shall miss Jimmy when I finish writing this book. I feel that I've come to know him as some kind of friend, some kind of maddening but fundamentally good-natured boy who wanted so much and got most of it before it could make any sense to him. He was an astonishing creature who operated purely on instinct and fashioned a cinematic presence that remains uniquely magnetic to this day. Catch up on his legend while you can.